Ninja Foodi Digital Air Fry Oven Cookbook

Quick, Delicious & Easy-to-Prepare Recipes for Your Family and Friends.

Include 3-Weeks Meal Plan to Start Your Daily Diet

Tracy Martinez

© **Copyright 2020 - All rights reserved.**

The content contained within this book may not be reproduced, duplicated or transmitted without direct written permission from the author or the publisher.

Under no circumstances will any blame or legal responsibility be held against the publisher, or author, for any damages, reparation, or monetary loss due to the information contained within this book, either directly or indirectly.

Legal Notice:

This book is copyright protected. It is only for personal use. You cannot amend, distribute, sell, use, quote or paraphrase any part, or the content within this book, without the consent of the author or publisher.

Disclaimer Notice:

Please note the information contained within this document is for educational and entertainment purposes only. All effort has been executed to present accurate, up to date, reliable, complete information. No warranties of any kind are declared or implied. Readers acknowledge that the author is not engaged in the rendering of legal, financial, medical or professional advice. The content within this book has been derived from various sources. Please consult a licensed professional before attempting any techniques outlined in this book.

By reading this document, the reader agrees that under no circumstances is the author responsible for any losses, direct or indirect, that are incurred as a result of the use of the information contained within this document, including, but not limited to, errors, omissions, or inaccuracies.

Table of Contents

Introduction 5
   Smart Cooking Programs 5
   Quick User Guide 5

Chapter 1: Breakfast Recipes 7
   Ham Brie Sandwich 7
   Breakfast Hash 8
   Breakfast Frittata 9
   Chile-Cheese Frittata 10
   Hasselback Potatoes 11
   Morning Bagels 12
   Egg Avocado Boats 13
   Breakfast Bombs 14

Chapter 2: Snacks and Appetizer Recipes 15
   Corn Dog Bites 15
   Beet Chips 16
   Cinnamon Apple Chips 17
   Shrimp Spring Rolls 18
   Curry Chickpeas 19
   Pork Dumplings 20
   Spanakopita Bites 21
   Pita Pizzas 23
   Corn on the Cob 24
   Calzones 25

   Sweet Potato Fries 26

Chapter 3: Poultry Mains Recipes 27
   Turkey Croquettes 27
   Thanksgiving Turkey Meal 28
   Italian Turkey Breast 29
   Turkey Meatloaf 30
   General Tso's Chicken 32
   Chicken Enchiladas 34
   Korean Chicken Wings 35
   Cheesy Chicken Nachos 37
   Chicken Stir-Fry 38
   Honey Lime Chicken Wings 39
   Chicken Tenders 40
   Chicken, Sweet Potatoes and Broccoli 41
   Chicken Sheet Pan Meal 42
   Turkey Ham Casserole 43

Chapter 4: Beef, Pork, and Lamb Recipes 45
   Italian Pasta Bake 45
   Sausage Casserole 46
   Christmas Casserole 47
   Holiday Ham 48
   Pork Meatballs 49
   Cauliflower Pork Casserole 50

Balsamic Pork Veggie Meal 51

Sheet Pan Pork with Apples 52

Lamb Sirloin Steak 53

Masala Chops 54

Lamb Chops with Garlic Sauce 55

Herbed Lamb Chops 56

Steak Bites Mushrooms 57

Glazed Steaks 58

Bacon Meatloaf 59

Chapter 5: Fish & Seafood Recipes 60

Buttered Salmon 60

Herbed Salmon 61

Glazed Salmon 62

Ranch Tilapia 63

Seasoned Catfish 64

Cod Parcel 65

Crusted Sole 66

Sweet & Tangy Herring 67

Lemony Shrimp 68

Halibut & Shrimp with Pasta 69

Herbed Scallops 70

Prawn Burgers 71

Chapter 6: Vegetable & Sides Recipes. 72

Green Beans & Mushroom Casserole 72

Potato Gratin 73

Veggie Ratatouille 74

Vegetarian Loaf 75

Veggie Kabobs 77

Stuffed Pumpkin 78

Basil Tomatoes 79

Parmesan Asparagus 80

Spicy Butternut Squash 81

Garlicky Brussels Sprout 82

Glazed Mushrooms 83

Chapter 7: Dessert Recipes 84

Banana Split 84

Nutty Pears 85

Glazed Figs 86

Citrus Mousse 87

Chocolate Pudding 88

Red Velvet Cupcakes 89

Chocolate Mug Cake 90

Plum Crisp 91

Vanilla Cheesecake 92

3 Weeks Meal Plan: 93

Week 1 93

Week 2 94

Week 3 96

Conclusion 98

Introduction

If you are looking for the ultimate kitchen companion that could bake, Air Fry, toast, dehydrate, and broil a variety of food all in one place, then Ninja Foodi Digital Air Fry Oven is the right fit for you. This advance Air Fry oven is not only multipurpose but also saves much space on your kitchen counter due to its smart flip design. Imagine, instead of having a toaster, an Air Fryer, and an oven separately lying on your kitchen shelf, you will have one single appliance which can do all of that with much efficiency. This 8-in-1 multipurpose Ninja oven is extremely user-friendly and gives its users complete control over both the cooking temperature and time. And this Ninja Foodi digital Air Fry oven cookbook is about to bring you all the irresistibly delicious recipes that you can cook in your new Ninja digital Air Fryer oven.

Smart Cooking Programs

The Ninja Foodi Digital Air fryer oven offers eight different cooking modes. It's a powerful heating system that runs on 1800, watt cooks food evenly and in a short time. The oven has the following cooking modes:

- Air Fry
- Air Roast
- Air Broil
- Bake
- Dehydrate
- Keep Warm
- Toast
- Bagel

After selecting the desired cooking mode, the cooking time and temperature can be selected using the rotating dial. The appliance automatically preheats once given instructions. For toasting, the user can select the number of slices and the level of darkness as well.

Quick User Guide

If you are completely new to this appliance, then here is how you can cook using its different cooking functions:

1. First, check all the components of the appliance and see if they all intact and in good shape.
2. To use the appliance for the first time, clean or wash its cooking accessories like the baking pan, sheet pan, and Air Fryer basket and let them completely dry.
3. Now plug in the device and press the "Power button" given on the control panel.
4. After pressing this button, the LED will light up and indicate the device is one.
5. Place the crumb tray at the bottom of the oven.

6. The Ninja Foodi digital Air Fry oven quickly preheats itself, so it is recommended to place the food inside and then set the mode, time, and temperature accordingly. Or at least keep the food ready to place inside the oven when it is preheated.
7. Place the prepared food inside and close the lid or door of the Ninja Foodi digital Air Fry oven.
8. To do so, first select the cooking mode. Rotate the dial, and it will switch between the modes. Stop rotating the dial when the blue light appears beside your desired mode.
9. After selecting the function, it's time to change the temperature and time settings.
10. To change the cooking time, first press the "Time" button and then rotate the dial to increase or decrease the number of minutes.
11. Similarly, to change the temperature, press the "Temp" button and rotate the dial to adjust the temperature according.
12. It is to note here that the "Time" button is also used to select the number of "Slices" when the oven is running on the "Toast" and "Bagel" mode, and the "Temp" button is used to set the level of "darkness" of the toasts on the given modes.
13. Initiate Cooking:
14. When the mode, temp, and time are adjusted, the device is ready to use.
15. For Baking, Air Frying, Air Roasting, and Broiling, the device takes some time to preheat.
16. It starts to preheat when the Dial is pressed to start the cooking.
17. At this point, the Led screen will show PRE in red color, and the timer does not start ticking until the PRE sign disappears and the device is preheated.
18. Once it is preheated, the device beeps to indicate that it will now automatically start cooking, and its timer will start running.
19. When the food is cooked, the device keeps it warm until you are ready to remove it from the oven.

Chapter 1: Breakfast Recipes

Ham Brie Sandwich

Prep Time: 15 minutes.
Cook Time: 10 minutes.
Serves: 2

Ingredients:

- 2 teaspoons butter salted
- 2 bread slices
- 2 ham slices
- 1 tablespoon blueberry BBQ sauce
- 3 oz. brie cheese, sliced

Preparation:

1. Place the bread slices on the working surface and top them with butter.
2. Add ham and brie slices on top of one bread slice and place the other side on top with its buttered side down.
3. Place this sandwich in the baking tray of the Ninja Foodi Digital Air Fryer oven.
4. Transfer the sandwich to the Ninja Foodi Digital Air Fryer Oven and close the door.
5. Select "Air Crisp" mode by rotating the dial.
6. Press the TEMP button and change the value to 375 degrees F.
7. Press the TIME button and change the value to 10 minutes, then press START to begin cooking.
8. Flip the sandwich after 5 minutes.
9. Slice and serve warm.

Serving Suggestion: Serve the cheese sandwiches with crispy bacon on the side.

Variation Tip: Add a layer of garlic mayonnaise to the sandwich before cooking.

Nutritional Information Per Serving:

Calories 284 | Fat 7.9g | Sodium 704mg | Carbs 46g | Fiber 3.6g | Sugar 6g | Protein 18g

Breakfast Hash

Prep Time: 15 minutes.
Cook Time: 20 minutes.
Serves: 4

Ingredients:

- 1/4 cup unsalted butter, melted
- 1 teaspoon paprika
- 1 ¾ cups russet potatoes, peeled and chopped
- 3/4 cup cooked kielbasa, chopped
- 1 small yellow onion, peeled, chopped
- 1 teaspoon salt

Preparation:

1. Toss potatoes, kielbasa, and onion in a large bowl.
2. Whisk melted butter, salt, and paprika in a small bowl.
3. Pour this mixture over the veggies and toss well to coat.
4. Spread the veggies in the Ninja sheet pan.
5. Transfer the sheet pan to the Ninja Foodi Digital Air Fryer Oven and close the door.
6. Select the "Bake" mode by rotating the dial.
7. Press the TEMP button and change the value to 400 degrees F.
8. Press the TIME button and change the value to 20 minutes, then press START to begin cooking.
9. Toss the veggies once cooked halfway through.
10. Serve warm.

Serving Suggestion: Serve the breakfast hash with crumbled crispy bacon on top and warm bread on the side

Variation Tip: Add chopped carrots and broccoli to the hash.

Nutritional Information Per Serving:

Calories 214 | Fat 5.1g | Sodium 231mg | Carbs 31g | Fiber 5g | Sugar 2.1g | Protein 17g

Breakfast Frittata

Prep Time: 15 minutes.

Cook Time: 12 minutes.

Serves: 4

Ingredients:

- ¼ lb. breakfast sausage, cooked and crumbled
- 4 eggs, beaten
- ½ cup Cheddar-Monterey Jack cheese, shredded
- 2 tablespoons red bell pepper, diced
- 1 green onion, chopped
- 1 pinch cayenne pepper
- Cooking spray

Preparation:

1. Beat eggs in a bowl and stir in cayenne, bell pepper, onion, and cheese.
2. Mix well and pour the egg-mixture into 6x2 inches baking pan.
3. Transfer the baking pan to the Ninja Foodi Digital Air Fryer Oven and close the door.
4. Select the "Bake" mode by rotating the dial.
5. Press the TEMP button and change the value to 400 degrees F.
6. Press the TIME button and change the value to 12 minutes, then press START to begin cooking.
7. Slice and serve warm.

Serving Suggestion: Serve the frittata with toasted French bread slices

Variation Tip: Sausage can be replaced with chopped ham slices.

Nutritional Information Per Serving:

Calories 387 | Fat 6g |Sodium 154mg | Carbs 37.4g | Fiber 2.9g | Sugar 15g | Protein 15g

Chile-Cheese Frittata

Prep Time: 15 minutes.

Cook Time: 12 minutes.

Serves: 4

Ingredients:

- Cooking spray
- 4 eggs
- 3 tablespoons heavy cream
- 2 bacon slices, cooked and crumbled
- ½ cup Jack cheese, shredded
- ¼ cup green chiles, chopped
- 3 tablespoons tomatoes, diced
- 2 tablespoons onion, chopped
- Salt and black pepper, to taste

Preparation:

1. Whisk eggs with cream, bacon, cheese, green chiles, tomatoes, onion, black pepper, and salt in a bowl.
2. Pour this egg mixture into the Ninja baking pan.
3. Transfer the baking pan to the Ninja Foodi Digital Air Fryer Oven and close the door.
4. Select the "Bake" mode by rotating the dial.
5. Press the TEMP button and change the value to 400 degrees F.
6. Press the TIME button and change the value to 12 minutes, then press START to begin cooking.

Serving Suggestion: Serve this frittata with crispy bread toasts.

Variation Tip: Add crumbled sausage to the egg-batter.

Nutritional Information Per Serving:

Calories 304 | Fat 32g |Sodium 890mg | Carbs 4.3g | Fiber 4g | Sugar 8g | Protein 25g

Hasselback Potatoes

Prep Time: 15 minutes.
Cook Time: 15 minutes.
Serves: 4

Ingredients:

- 4 potatoes
- Olive oil, to rub

Preparation:

1. Scrub the potatoes and cut 1/4inch apart slits in each potato while leaving 3/8 inch from the base.
2. Rub the potatoes with olive oil and place them in the Ninja Sheet pan.
3. Transfer the sheet pan to the Ninja Foodi Digital Air Fryer Oven and close the door.
4. Select "Air Crisp" mode by rotating the dial.
5. Press the TEMP button and change the value to 400 degrees F.
6. Press the TIME button and change the value to 15 minutes, then press START to begin cooking.
7. Serve warm.

Serving Suggestion: Serve the potatoes with cheese and bacon toppings.

Variation Tip: Insert a slice of tomato, cheese, and zucchini into the slits of potatoes before baking.

Nutritional Information Per Serving:
Calories 312 | Fat 25g | Sodium 132mg | Carbs 44g | Fiber 3.9g | Sugar 3g | Protein 18.9g

Morning Bagels

Prep Time: 15 minutes.
Cook Time: 9 minutes.
Serves: 6

Ingredients:

- 1 cup self-rising flour
- 1 cup Greek yogurt
- 1/2 cup cream cheese, whipped
- 2 tablespoons cinnamon and sugar
- Toasted sesame seeds

Preparation:

1. Mix flour with Greek yogurt and cream cheese in a bowl.
2. Divide the dough into 6 equal pieces and roll them into a ball.
3. Roll each of the six dough balls into a rope and shape each into a bagel.
4. Place the bagels in the Ninja Air Fryer basket.
5. Transfer the basket to the Ninja Foodi Digital Air Fryer Oven and close the door.
6. Select "Air Crisp" mode by rotating the dial.
7. Press the TEMP button and change the value to 325 degrees F.
8. Press the TIME button and change the value to 9 minutes, then press START to begin cooking.
9. Flip the bagels once cooked halfway through, then resume cooking.
10. Coat the bagels with cinnamon, sugar, and sesame seeds.
11. Serve.

Serving Suggestion: Serve the bagels with fried eggs and crispy bacon.

Variation Tip: Add chopped pecans or walnuts to the batter.

Nutritional Information Per Serving:

Calories 331 | Fat 2.5g |Sodium 595mg | Carbs 69g | Fiber 12g | Sugar 12g | Protein 8.7g

Egg Avocado Boats

Prep Time: 15 minutes.
Cook Time: 12 minutes.
Serves: 2

Ingredients:

- 1 Avocado
- Salt, to taste
- Black pepper to taste
- Cooking spray
- 2 eggs

Preparation:

1. Slice the avocado in half, remove the pit and scoop a teaspoon of flesh from the center.
2. Crack one egg into each avocado and drizzle black pepper and salt on top.
3. Place the avocado in the Ninja Air Fryer basket and spray them with cooking spray.
4. Transfer the Air Fryer basket to the Ninja Foodi Digital Air Fryer Oven and close the door.
5. Select "Air Crisp" mode by rotating the dial.
6. Press the TEMP button and change the value to 390 degrees F.
7. Press the TIME button and change the value to 12 minutes, then press START to begin cooking.
8. Serve warm.

Serving Suggestion: Serve the avocado cups with crispy bacon on top.

Variation Tip: Top egg with fresh herbs or chopped bell pepper.

Nutritional Information Per Serving:
Calories 297 | Fat 15g | Sodium 202mg | Carbs 58.5g | Fiber 4g | Sugar 1g | Protein 7.3g

Breakfast Bombs

Prep Time: 15 minutes.
Cook Time: 19 minutes.
Serves: 4

Ingredients:

- 3 bacon slices
- 3 large eggs, beaten
- 1 oz. cream cheese, softened
- 1 tablespoon fresh chives. chopped
- 4 oz. whole-wheat pizza dough
- Cooking spray

Preparation:

1. Sauté bacon in a skillet for 10 minutes until crispy. Transfer it to a plate and allow it cool
2. Crumble the bacon in a bowl and crack eggs into the bowl.
3. Stir in chives and cream cheese. Then beat well.
4. Cook the egg-bacon mixture in a greased skillet for 5 minutes to get a scramble.
5. Divide the wheat dough into 4 pieces and spread each into a 5-inch circle.
6. Divide the egg mixture on top of the dough circles.
7. Brush the edges of the dough with water and bring the edges together, then pinch them together.
8. Place the balls in the baking tray, greased with cooking spray with their seam side down.
9. Transfer the baking tray to the Ninja Foodi Digital Air Fryer Oven and close the door.
10. Select "Air Crisp" mode by rotating the dial.
11. Press the TEMP button and change the value to 350 degrees F.
12. Press the TIME button and change the value to 9 minutes, then press START to begin cooking.
13. Flip the balls once cooked halfway through, then resume cooking.
14. Serve warm.

Serving Suggestion: Serve these bombs with your hot sauce or any other tangy sauce you like.

Variation Tip: Add sautéed ground chicken or pork to the egg filling.

Nutritional Information Per Serving:
Calories 305 | Fat 15g |Sodium 548mg | Carbs 26g | Fiber 2g | Sugar 1g | Protein 19g

Chapter 2: Snacks and Appetizer Recipes

Corn Dog Bites

Prep Time: 15 minutes.

Cook Time: 10 minutes.

Serves: 6

Ingredients:

- 2 beef hot dogs
- 12 craft sticks or bamboo skewers
- 1/2 cup all-purpose flour
- 2 large eggs, beaten
- 1 ½ cups crushed cornflakes cereal
- Cooking spray
- 8 teaspoons yellow mustard

Preparation:

1. Cut each hot dog into six small pieces and insert a craft stick into each piece.
2. Spread flour in one bowl, beat eggs in another bowl, and spread the cornflakes on a plate.
3. Dredge the hot dogs through the flour, dip each in the egg and then coat with the cornflakes.
4. Place the hot dog sticks in the Ninja baking tray and spray them with cooking spray.
5. Transfer the baking tray to the Ninja Foodi Digital Air Fryer Oven and close the door.
6. Select "Air Crisp" mode by rotating the dial.
7. Press the TEMP button and change the value to 375 degrees F.
8. Press the TIME button and change the value to 10 minutes, then press START to begin cooking.
9. Flip the corn dogs once cooked halfway through, then resume cooking.
10. Serve warm.

Serving Suggestion: Serve the corn dogs with tomato ketchup or cheese dip.

Variation Tip: Skip cornflakes and coat the corn dogs with breadcrumbs.

Nutritional Information Per Serving:

Calories 148 | Fat 22g | Sodium 350mg | Carbs 32.2g | Fiber 0.7g | Sugar 1g | Protein 4.3g

Beet Chips

Prep Time: 15 minutes.
Cook Time: 30 minutes.
Serves: 6

Ingredients:

- 3 red beets, peeled and sliced
- 2 teaspoons canola oil
- 3/4 teaspoon salt
- 1/4 teaspoon black pepper

Preparation:

1. Toss the beets with canola oil, black pepper, and salt in a bowl.
2. Spread the seasoned beet slice in the Ninja Air Fryer basket.
3. Transfer the basket to the Ninja Foodi Digital Air Fryer Oven and close the door.
4. Select "Air Crisp" mode by rotating the dial.
5. Press the TEMP button and change the value to 320 degrees F.
6. Press the TIME button and change the value to 30 minutes, then press START to begin cooking.
7. Toss the beets once cooked halfway through, then resume cooking.
8. Serve.

Serving Suggestion: Serve the chips with white cheese dip.

Variation Tip: Drizzle cinnamon ground on top before baking.

Nutritional Information Per Serving:

Calories 47 | Fat 2g | Sodium 48mg | Carbs 6g | Fiber 2g | Sugar 0g | Protein 1g

Cinnamon Apple Chips

Prep Time: 15 minutes.

Cook Time: 12 minutes.

Serves: 4

Ingredients:

- 1 (8-oz.) apple, sliced
- 1 teaspoon ground cinnamon
- 2 teaspoons canola oil
- Cooking spray
- 1/4 cup Greek yogurt
- 1 tablespoon almond butter
- 1 teaspoon honey

Preparation:

1. Toss apple slices with oil and cinnamon in a baking tray.
2. Spread the apple slices in the Ninja Air Fryer basket.
3. Transfer the basket to the Ninja Foodi Digital Air Fryer Oven and close the door.
4. Select "Air Crisp" mode by rotating the dial.
5. Press the TEMP button and change the value to 375 degrees F.
6. Press the TIME button and change the value to 12 minutes, then press START to begin cooking.
7. Toss the apple slices once cooked halfway through, then resume cooking.
8. Beat yogurt with honey and almond butter in a bowl.
9. Serve the apple chips with the yogurt dip.

Serving Suggestion: Serve the chips with apple sauce.

Variation Tip: Coat the apple slices with breadcrumbs before cooking.

Nutritional Information Per Serving:

Calories 104 | Fat 3g |Sodium 216mg | Carbs 17g | Fiber 3g | Sugar 4g | Protein 1g

Shrimp Spring Rolls

Prep Time: 15 minutes.
Cook Time: 9 minutes.
Serves: 4

Ingredients:

- 2 ½ tablespoons sesame oil
- 2 cups cabbage, shredded
- 1 cup carrots, julienned
- 1 cup red bell pepper, julienned
- 4 oz. raw shrimp, peeled, deveined, chopped
- 3/4 cup snow peas peeled, deveined
- 1/4 cup cilantro, chopped
- 1 tablespoon fresh lime juice
- 2 teaspoons fish sauce
- 1/4 teaspoon crushed red pepper
- 8 (8-inch-square) spring roll wrappers
- 1/2 cup sweet chili sauce

Preparation:

1. Sauté cabbage, bell pepper, and carrots with oil in a cooking pan for 2 minutes.
2. Allow the veggies to cool, then transfer to a bowl.
3. Stir in lime juice, cilantro, snow peas, shrimp, fish sauce, and crushed red pepper, then mix well.
4. Spread the spring roll wrappers on a working surface.
5. Divide the cabbage filling at the center of each wrapper.
6. Wet the edges of the wrappers, fold the top and bottom of each wrapper then roll them.
7. Place the shrimp spring rolls in the Ninja Air Fryer basket.
8. Transfer the basket to the Ninja Foodi Digital Air Fryer Oven and close the door.
9. Select "Air Crisp" mode by rotating the dial.
10. Press the TEMP button and change the value to 390 degrees F.
11. Press the TIME button and change the value to 7 minutes, then press START to begin cooking.
12. Flip the rolls once cooked halfway through, then resume cooking.
13. Serve the rolls with chili sauce.

Serving Suggestion: Serve the rolls with chili sauce or mayonnaise dip.

Variation Tip: Added shredded cheese to the spring roll filling.

Nutritional Information Per Serving:
Calories 180 | Fat 9g |Sodium 318mg | Carbs 19g | Fiber 5g | Sugar 3g | Protein 7g

Curry Chickpeas

Prep Time: 15 minutes.
Cook Time: 15 minutes.
Serves: 6

Ingredients:

- 1 (15-oz.) can chickpeas, drained
- 2 tablespoons red wine vinegar
- 2 tablespoons olive oil
- 2 teaspoons curry powder
- 1/2 teaspoon ground turmeric
- 1/4 teaspoon ground coriander
- 1/4 teaspoon ground cumin
- 1/4 teaspoon 1ground cinnamon
- 1/4 teaspoon salt
- 1/2 teaspoon Aleppo pepper

Preparation:

1. Slightly smash the chickpeas in a bowl with your hands only to remove their skins.
2. Add oil, vinegar, curry powder, coriander, turmeric, cinnamon, and cumin.
3. Toss well and spread the chickpeas in the Ninja Air Fryer basket.
4. Transfer the basket to the Ninja Foodi Digital Air Fryer Oven and close the door.
5. Select "Air Crisp" mode by rotating the dial.
6. Press the TEMP button and change the value to 400 degrees F.
7. Press the TIME button and change the value to 15 minutes, then press START to begin cooking.
8. Toss the chickpeas once cooked halfway through, then resume cooking.
9. Garnish with salt and Aleppo pepper.
10. Serve.

Serving Suggestion: Serve the chickpeas with crumbled nacho chips on top and a cream cheese dip on the side.

Variation Tip: Toss chickpeas with shredded parmesan before cooking.

Nutritional Information Per Serving:
Calories 173 | Fat 8g |Sodium 146mg | Carbs 18g | Fiber 5g | Sugar 1g | Protein 7g

Pork Dumplings

Prep Time: 15 minutes.
Cook Time: 21 minutes.
Serves: 9

Ingredients:

- 1 teaspoon canola oil
- 4 cups bok choy, chopped
- 1 tablespoon fresh ginger, chopped
- 1 tablespoon garlic, chopped
- 4 oz. ground pork
- 1/4 teaspoon crushed red pepper
- 18 (3 1/2-inch-square) dumpling wrappers
- Cooking spray
- 2 tablespoons rice vinegar
- 2 teaspoons soy sauce
- 1 teaspoon toasted sesame oil
- 1/2 teaspoon packed brown sugar
- 1 tablespoon scallions, chopped

Preparation:

1. Sauté bok coy with canola oil in a skillet for 8 minutes.
2. Stir in garlic and ginger and cook for 1 minute.
3. Transfer the bok choy to a plate lined with a paper towel.
4. Mix bok choy mixture with ground pork and red pepper in a medium bowl.
5. Spread the dumpling wrappers on the working surface.
6. Divide the pork mixture at the center of each wrapper.
7. Wet the edges of the wrappers with water and fold the wrappers in half.
8. Pinch the edges of each wrapper and place them in the Ninja Air Fryer basket.
9. Transfer the basket to the Ninja Foodi Digital Air Fryer Oven and close the door.
10. Select "Air Crisp" mode by rotating the dial.
11. Press the TEMP button and change the value to 375 degrees F.
12. Press the TIME button and change the value to 12 minutes, then press START to begin cooking.
13. Flip the dumplings once cooked halfway through, then resume cooking.
14. Meanwhile, mix rice vinegar, sesame oil, soy sauce, scallions and brown sugar in a bowl.
15. Serve the pork dumplings with the prepared sauce.

Serving Suggestion: Serve the dumplings with chili sauce or mayo dip.

Variation Tip: Add shredded cheese to the filling.

Nutritional Information Per Serving:

Calories 140 | Fat 5g | Sodium 244mg | Carbs 16g | Fiber 1g | Sugar 1g | Protein 17g

Spanakopita Bites

Prep Time: 15 minutes.
Cook Time: 17 minutes.
Serves: 6

Ingredients:

- 1 (10-oz.) package spinach leaves
- 2 tablespoons water
- 1/4 cup cottage cheese
- 1 oz. feta cheese, crumbled
- 2 tablespoons Parmesan cheese, grated
- 1 large egg white
- 1 teaspoon lemon zest
- 1 teaspoon dried oregano
- 1/4 teaspoon black pepper
- 1/4 teaspoon salt
- 1/8 teaspoon cayenne pepper
- 4 (13x18 inches) sheets frozen phyllo dough, thawed
- 1 tablespoon olive oil
- Cooking spray

Preparation:

1. Boil spinach in a large pot with boiling pot for 5 minutes, then drain.
2. Mix the spinach with cottage cheese, Parmesan, feta cheese, zest, egg white, oregano, salt, black pepper, and cayenne pepper in a medium bowl.
3. Spread 1 phyllo sheet on a working surface brush the top with oil.
4. Place the second sheet on top and brush it with oil and repeat the layers with the remaining two sheets.
5. Cut these sheets into eight (2 ¼ inch wide) strips. Cut each strip in half and add a tablespoon of the filling at a short end of each strip.
6. Fold the corner covering the filling and make a triangle, then pinch the edges to seal the filling.
7. Place half of the triangles in the Ninja Air Fryer basket and spray them with cooking spray.
8. Transfer the basket to the Ninja Foodi Digital Air Fryer Oven and close the door.
9. Select "Air Crisp" mode by rotating the dial.
10. Press the TEMP button and change the value to 375 degrees F.

11. Press the TIME button and change the value to 12 minutes, then press START to begin cooking.
12. Flip the triangles once cooked halfway through, then resume cooking.
13. Cooking the remaining triangles in the same way.
14. Serve warm.

Serving Suggestion: Serve the Spanakopita with spinach or cream cheese dip.

Variation Tip: Add shredded cooked chicken to the spinach filling.

Nutritional Information Per Serving:
Calories 82 | Fat 4g |Sodium 232mg | Carbs 7g | Fiber 1g | Sugar 0g | Protein 4g

Pita Pizzas

Prep Time: 15 minutes.
Cook Time: 5 minutes.
Serves: 2

Ingredients:

- 1/4 cup marinara sauce
- 2 whole-wheat pita rounds
- 1 cup baby spinach leaves
- 1 plum tomato, sliced
- 1 garlic clove, sliced
- 1 oz. mozzarella cheese, shredded
- 1/4 oz. Parmigiano-Reggiano cheese shaved

Preparation:

1. Place the pita bread in the Ninja baking tray.
2. Spread the marinara sauce on top of both the pita bread.
3. Divide the spinach leaves, tomato slices, garlic, and both kinds of cheese.
4. Transfer the tray to the Ninja Foodi Digital Air Fryer Oven and close the door.
5. Select the "Bake" mode by rotating the dial.
6. Press the TEMP button and change the value to 350 degrees F.
7. Press the TIME button and change the value to 5 minutes, then press START to begin cooking.
8. Serve warm.

Serving Suggestion: Serve the pizza with tomato sauce or mayo dip.

Variation Tip: Add pepperoni and olive slices to the toppings.

Nutritional Information Per Serving:

Calories 229 | Fat 5g |Sodium 510mg | Carbs 37g | Fiber 5g | Sugar 4g | Protein 11g

Corn on the Cob

Prep Time: 15 minutes.
Cook Time: 14 minutes.
Serves: 4

Ingredients:

- 4 corn ears, shucked
- Cooking spray
- 1 ½ tablespoon unsalted butter
- 2 teaspoons garlic, chopped
- 1 teaspoon lime zest
- 1 tablespoon lime juice
- ½ teaspoon salt
- ½ teaspoon black pepper
- 2 tablespoons chopped fresh cilantro

Preparation:

1. Place the corn cobs in the Ninja Air Fryer basket and spray them with cooking spray.
2. Transfer the basket to the Ninja Foodi Digital Air Fryer Oven and close the door.
3. Select "Air Crisp" mode by rotating the dial.
4. Press the TEMP button and change the value to 400 degrees F.
5. Press the TIME button and change the value to 14 minutes, then press START to begin cooking.
6. Flip the corn cobs once cooked halfway through, then resume cooking.
7. Mix butter with salt, black pepper, cilantro, lime zest, lime juice, and garlic in a bowl.
8. Pour this mixture over the corn cobs.
9. Serve warm.

Serving Suggestion: Serve the corn cobs with garlic butter.

Variation Tip: Drizzle paprika on top for more spice.

Nutritional Information Per Serving:

Calories 201 | Fat 7g | Sodium 269mg | Carbs 35g | Fiber 4g | Sugar 12g | Protein 6g

Calzones

Prep Time: 15 minutes.
Cook Time: 14 minutes.
Serves: 4

Ingredients:

- 1 teaspoon olive oil
- 1/4 cup red onion, chopped
- 3 oz. baby spinach leaves
- 1/3 cup marinara sauce
- 2 oz. cooked chicken breast, shredded
- 6 oz. whole-wheat pizza dough
- 1 ½ oz. mozzarella cheese, shredded
- Cooking spray

Preparation:

1. Sauté onion with oil in a skillet for 2 minutes, then add spinach.
2. Cook for 1 ½ minute, then remove it from the heat.
3. Add chicken and marinara sauce, then mix well.
4. Cut the dough into 4 pieces and roll each piece into 6 inches circle.
5. Divide the spinach filling at the center of each dough piece.
6. Top the filling with the cheese and fold the dough in half.
7. Crimp the edges of each calzone and place them in the Ninja Air Fryer basket.
8. Transfer the basket to the Ninja Foodi Digital Air Fryer Oven and close the door.
9. Select "Air Crisp" mode by rotating the dial.
10. Press the TEMP button and change the value to 325 degrees F.
11. Press the TIME button and change the value to 12 minutes, then press START to begin cooking.
12. Flip the calzones once cooked halfway through, then resume cooking.
13. Serve warm.

Serving Suggestion: Serve the calzones with chili garlic sauce.

Variation Tip: Add pepperoni and sliced olives to the filling.

Nutritional Information Per Serving:
Calories 348 | Fat 12g | Sodium 710mg | Carbs 44g | Fiber 5g | Sugar 3g | Protein 11g

Sweet Potato Fries

Prep Time: 15 minutes.
Cook Time: 10 minutes.
Serves: 6

Ingredients:

- 3 sweet potatoes, cut into fries
- 2 tablespoons olive oil
- 1/2 teaspoon salt
- 1/4 teaspoon black pepper
- 1/4 teaspoon paprika
- 1/2 teaspoon garlic powder
- Parsley, to garnish

Preparation:

1. Toss the sweet potatoes with olive oil, salt, black pepper, paprika, and garlic powder in a bowl.
2. Spread the sweet potatoes in the Ninja Air Fryer basket and spray them with cooking spray.
3. Transfer the basket to the Ninja Foodi Digital Air Fryer Oven and close the door.
4. Select "Air Crisp" mode by rotating the dial.
5. Press the TEMP button and change the value to 400 degrees F.
6. Press the TIME button and change the value to 10 minutes, then press START to begin cooking.
7. Toss the fries once cooked halfway through, then resume cooking.
8. Serve warm.

Serving Suggestion: Serve the chips with tomato ketchup.

Variation Tip: Coat the sweet potatoes in breadcrumbs before cooking.

Nutritional Information Per Serving:

Calories 175 | Fat 16g | Sodium 255mg | Carbs 31g | Fiber 1.2g | Sugar 5g | Protein 4.1g

Chapter 3: Poultry Mains Recipes

Turkey Croquettes

Prep Time: 15 minutes.
Cook Time: 10 minutes.
Serves: 4

Ingredients:

- 1 cup turkey breast, diced
- 2 large eggs
- 1/2 cup potato starch
- 1 cup Japanese style panko
- 1 cup turkey gravy
- 1/2 cup leftover cranberry sauce

Preparation:

1. Beat eggs in a bowl, spread potato starch in another bowl and add panko to a shallow tray.
2. Coat the turkey cubes with potato starch then dip in the eggs and then coat with the panko.
3. Place the turkey cubes in the Ninja Air Fryer basket and spray them with cooking spray.
4. Transfer the basket to the Ninja Foodi Digital Air Fryer Oven and close the door.
5. Select "Air Crisp" mode by rotating the dial.
6. Press the TEMP button and change the value to 380 degrees F.
7. Press the TIME button and change the value to 10 minutes, then press START to begin cooking.
8. Serve with gravy and cranberry sauce.

Serving Suggestion: Serve the turkey croquettes with a kale salad on the side.

Variation Tip: Coat the croquettes with coconut shreds.

Nutritional Information Per Serving:
Calories 235 | Fat 25g | Sodium 122mg | Carbs 23g | Fiber 0.4g | Sugar 1g | Protein 33g

Thanksgiving Turkey Meal

Prep Time: 15 minutes.
Cook Time: 20 minutes.
Serves: 8

Ingredients:

- 1 teaspoon salt
- 1 teaspoon dried thyme
- 1 teaspoon ground rosemary
- 1/2 teaspoon black pepper
- 1/2 teaspoon dried sage
- 1/2 teaspoon garlic powder
- 1/2 teaspoon paprika
- 1/2 teaspoon dark brown sugar
- 2 1/2 lbs. bone-in, skin-on turkey breast
- Olive oil, for brushing

Preparation:

1. Mix salt, thyme, rosemary, black pepper, sage, garlic powder, paprika, and sugar in a bowl.
2. Rub oil and spice blend over the turkey breast.
3. Place the turkey breast the Ninja sheet pan.
4. Transfer the sheet pan to the Ninja Foodi Digital Air Fryer Oven and close the door.
5. Select "Air Roast" mode by rotating the dial.
6. Press the TEMP button and change the value to 360 degrees F.
7. Press the TIME button and change the value to 20 minutes, then press START to begin cooking.
8. Slice and serve warm.

Serving Suggestion: Serve the turkey with roasted green beans and mashed potatoes.

Variation Tip: Place bacon slices on top of the turkey before baking.

Nutritional Information Per Serving:

Calories 235 | Fat 5g |Sodium 422mg | Carbs 16g | Fiber 0g | Sugar 1g | Protein 25g

Italian Turkey Breast

Prep Time: 15 minutes.
Cook Time: 55 minutes.
Serves: 8

Ingredients:

- 1 (4 lbs.) bone-in turkey breast, ribs removed
- 1½ cups Italian dressing
- ¼ cup Worcestershire sauce

Preparation:

1. Cut out the ribs from the turkey breast and rub it with Italian seasoning and Worcestershire sauce.
2. Place the turkey on a plate, cover, and refrigerate for 1 hour for marination.
3. Place the marinated turkey breasts in the Ninja Air Fryer basket.
4. Transfer the basket to the Ninja Foodi Digital Air Fryer Oven and close the door.
5. Select "Air Crisp" mode by rotating the dial.
6. Press the TEMP button and change the value to 350 degrees F.
7. Press the TIME button and change the value to 20 minutes, then press START to begin cooking.
8. Flip the turkey breast and continue cooking for another 35 minutes.
9. Slice and serve warm.

Serving Suggestion: Serve the turkey breast with roasted veggies.

Variation Tip: wrap the turkey breast with bacon slices before baking.

Nutritional Information Per Serving:
Calories 369 | Fat 14g | Sodium 442mg | Carbs 13.3g | Fiber 0.4g | Sugar 2g | Protein 32.3g

Turkey Meatloaf

Prep Time: 15 minutes.
Cook Time: 32 minutes.
Serves: 6

Ingredients:

- Cooking spray
- 1/4 cup water
- Salt, as desired
- 1 lb. uncooked ground turkey
- 1/3 cup panko bread crumbs
- 2 potatoes, peeled, cut into 1-inch pieces
- 1 yellow onion, peeled, grated
- 1 garlic clove, peeled, grated
- 1 egg
- 1/4 cup Colby-Jack cheese, diced
- 1/3 cup ketchup
- Ground black pepper, to taste
- 1 package (12 oz.) fresh green beans
- 1 tablespoon olive oil
- 1/3 cup whole milk
- 1 tablespoon butter

Preparation:

1. Add potatoes onto a large piece of aluminum foil and season them with cooking spray and salt.
2. Wrap the potatoes and place the packet in the Ninja sheet pan.
3. Mix turkey with egg, cheese, half the ketchup, black pepper, salt, egg, garlic, onion, and breadcrumbs in a bowl.
4. Divide the meatloaves mixture into four portions.
5. Shape each portion into a mini-loaf, brush the ketchup on top and place them in the sheet pan.
6. Transfer the sheet pan to the Ninja Foodi Digital Air Fryer Oven and close the door.
7. Select "Air Roast" mode by rotating the dial.
8. Press the TEMP button and change the value to 400 degrees F.
9. Press the TIME button and change the value to 15 minutes, then press START to begin cooking.
10. Meanwhile, toss green beans with salt, black pepper and olive oil in a bowl.

11. Place green beans in the sheet pan and return it to the Ninja Digital Air Fryer oven.
12. Continue cooking for another 17 minutes on the same mode and temperature.
13. Unwrap the potatoes and add them to a bowl.
14. Mash the potatoes and add milk, black pepper, salt and milk.
15. Mix well and serve the turkey loaves and green beans.
16. Serve warm.

Serving Suggestion: Serve the meatloaf with fresh cucumber and couscous salad.

Variation Tip: Wrap the meatloaves with bacon slices before cooking.

Nutritional Information Per Serving:
Calories 453 | Fat 2.4g |Sodium 216mg | Carbs 18g | Fiber 2.3g | Sugar 1.2g | Protein 23.2g

General Tso's Chicken

Prep Time: 15 minutes.
Cook Time: 17 minutes.
Serves: 4

Ingredients:

- 1 large egg
- 1 lb. chicken thighs, cut into chunks
- 1/3 cup 2 teaspoons cornstarch
- ¼ teaspoon salt
- ¼ teaspoon ground white pepper
- 7 tablespoons chicken broth
- 2 tablespoons soy sauce
- 2 tablespoons ketchup
- 2 teaspoons sugar
- 2 teaspoons rice vinegar
- 1 ½ tablespoon canola oil
- 4 chiles de árbol, chopped
- 1 tablespoon fresh ginger, chopped
- 1 tablespoon garlic, chopped
- 2 tablespoons green onion, sliced
- 1 teaspoon toasted sesame oil
- ½ teaspoon toasted sesame seeds

Preparation:

1. Beat egg in a bowl and add chicken to coat well.
2. Mix 1/3 cup cornstarch with black pepper and salt in a bowl.
3. Coat the chicken with the cornstarch mixture.
4. Place the chicken in the Ninja Air Fryer basket and spray with cooking spray.
5. Transfer the basket to the Ninja Foodi Digital Air Fryer Oven and close the door.
6. Select "Air Roast" mode by rotating the dial.
7. Press the TEMP button and change the value to 400 degrees F.
8. Press the TIME button and change the value to 16 minutes, then press START to begin cooking.
9. Flip the chicken once cooked halfway through and resume cooking.
10. Mix 2 teaspoons with broth, soy sauce, sugar, rice vinegar, ketchup, and 2 teaspoons cornstarch in a bowl.
11. Sauté chiles with oil in a skillet for 30 seconds.

12. Stir in ginger and garlic then sauté for 30 seconds.
13. Add cornstarch sauté to the garlic and cook until the mixture thickens.
14. Stir in air fried chicken then mix well.
15. Garnish with sesame oil, sesame seeds and green onion.
16. Serve warm.

Serving Suggestion: Serve the chicken with fresh herbs on top and a bowl of steamed rice.

Variation Tip: Use honey or maple syrup to the sauce if not using ketchup.

Nutritional Information Per Serving:
Calories 302 | Fat 13g |Sodium 611mg | Carbs 18g | Fiber 0g | Sugar g4 | Protein 26g

Chicken Enchiladas

Prep Time: 15 minutes.
Cook Time: 15 minutes.
Serves: 12

Ingredients:

- 12 corn tortillas
- 1½ cups Mexican chicken, shredded
- 2 cups enchilada sauce
- 1½ cups Mexican cheese, shredded

Preparation:

1. Spread six tortillas in the Ninja sheet pan and spray them with cooking spray.
2. Transfer the sheet pan to the Ninja Foodi Digital Air Fryer Oven and close the door.
3. Select "Air Crisp" mode by rotating the dial.
4. Press the TEMP button and change the value to 425 degrees F.
5. Press the TIME button and change the value to 5 minutes, then press START to begin cooking.
6. Air Fry the remaining tortillas in the same manner.
7. Mix shredded chicken with enchilada sauce in a bowl.
8. Divide the filling in each tortilla then place the stuffed tortillas in the Ninja sheet pan.
9. Drizzle sheet on top of each tortilla.
10. Transfer the sheet pan to the Ninja Foodi Digital Air Fryer Oven and close the door.
11. Select the "Bake" mode by rotating the dial.
12. Press the TEMP button and change the value to 325 degrees F.
13. Press the TIME button and change the value to 15 minutes, then press START to begin cooking.
14. Serve warm.

Serving Suggestion: Serve the chicken enchiladas with toasted bread slices.

Variation Tip: Add corn kernels to the chicken filling.

Nutritional Information Per Serving:
Calories 354 | Fat 25g |Sodium 412mg | Carbs 22.3g | Fiber 0.2g | Sugar 1g | Protein 28.3g

Korean Chicken Wings

Prep Time: 15 minutes.

Cook Time: 10 minutes.

Serves: 6

Ingredients:

- 2 lbs. chicken wings
- 2 tablespoons of rice wine
- 1 teaspoon onion powder
- 1 teaspoon garlic powder
- 1 teaspoon sea salt
- 1/4 teaspoon ginger powder
- Black pepper, to taste

Soy Garlic Sauce

- 3 tablespoons soy sauce
- 2 tablespoons water
- 2 tablespoons of rice wine
- 2 tablespoons brown sugar
- 2 tablespoons honey
- 1/2 tablespoon ginger, minced
- ½ tablespoon garlic, minced
- 1 teaspoon ground black peppers
- 1 oz. green onions, chopped
- 3 dried chilies, chopped
- 2 teaspoons corn starch
- 2 teaspoons water

Sweet Spicy Sauce

- 1 ½ tablespoons ketchup
- 1 tablespoon Korean chili paste
- 2 tablespoons honey
- 2 tablespoons brown sugar
- 1 tablespoon soy sauce
- 1 tablespoon minced garlic
- ½ tablespoons sesame oil

Garnish

- Sesame seeds

- Green onion, sliced

Preparation:

1. Dip the chicken wings in the rice wine and soak for 5 minutes.
2. Mix black peppers, ginger powder, salt, garlic powder and onion powder in a bowl.
3. Add the chicken wings and coat them well with the spices.
4. Spread the chicken wings in the Ninja Air Fryer basket and spray them with the cooking spray.
5. Transfer the basket to the Ninja Foodi Digital Air Fryer Oven and close the door.
6. Select "Air Crisp" mode by rotating the dial.
7. Press the TEMP button and change the value to 400 degrees F.
8. Press the TIME button and change the value to 10 minutes, then press START to begin cooking.
9. Toss the chicken once cooked halfway through.
10. Meanwhile, mix all the soy garlic sauce in a cooking pot and cook for 2 minutes, then allow it to cool.
11. Mix the sweet and spicy sauce ingredients in a bowl.
12. Add the chicken wings to the soy garlic sauce then mix well.
13. Pour in the sweet and spicy sauce then mix well.
14. Serve.

Serving Suggestion: Serve the wings with white rice or vegetable chow Mein.

Variation Tip: Coat or dust the wings with flour for a crispy texture.

Nutritional Information Per Serving:
Calories 297 | Fat 14g | Sodium 364mg | Carbs 8g | Fiber 1g | Sugar 3g | Protein 32g

Cheesy Chicken Nachos

Prep Time: 15 minutes.
Cook Time: 25 minutes.
Serves: 4

Ingredients:

- 1 lb. chicken breasts, cut into cubes
- 1 tablespoon olive oil
- 8 oz. tortilla chips
- 1 can (15 ½ oz.) black beans
- 2 cups cheddar cheese, shredded
- 1 cup Mexican blend cheese, shredded

Nacho seasoning

- 1 tablespoon fresh lemon juice
- 1 tablespoon fresh lime juice
- 1 teaspoon ground cumin
- ¼ cup cilantro, chopped
- 1 teaspoon onion powder
- 2 teaspoons chili powder
- 1 teaspoon salt

Preparation:

1. Mix all the nacho seasoning ingredients in a bowl.
2. Toss chicken with nacho seasoning and oil in the Ninja sheet pan.
3. Transfer the sheet pan to the Ninja Foodi Digital Air Fryer Oven and close the door.
4. Select "Air Roast" mode by rotating the dial.
5. Press the TEMP button and change the value to 350 degrees F.
6. Press the TIME button and change the value to 15 minutes, then press START to begin cooking.
7. Spread the tortilla chips in a sheet pan and top them with chicken, black beans, and cheese.
8. Transfer the basket to the Ninja Foodi Digital Air Fryer Oven and close the door.
9. Select "Air Roast" mode by rotating the dial.
10. Press the TEMP button and change the value to 350 degrees F.
11. Press the TIME button and change the value to 10 minutes, then press START to begin cooking.
12. Serve warm.

Serving Suggestion: Serve the nachos with avocado guacamole.

Variation Tip: Add corn kernels to the nachos topping.

Nutritional Information Per Serving:
Calories 352 | Fat 14g | Sodium 220mg | Carbs 16g | Fiber 0.2g | Sugar 1g | Protein 26g

Chicken Stir-Fry

Prep Time: 15 minutes.
Cook Time: 30 minutes.
Serves: 2

Ingredients:

- 1 lb. chicken breasts, cut into cubes
- 1 red bell pepper, sliced
- 1 yellow bell pepper, sliced
- 1 orange bell pepper, sliced
- 2 carrots, sliced
- ½ cup stir-fry sauce
- 1 head broccoli, cut into florets
- 1 teaspoon sesame seeds

Preparation:

1. Toss chicken, carrots, and peppers in the Ninja sheet pan.
2. Transfer the sheet pan to the Ninja Foodi Digital Air Fryer Oven and close the door.
3. Select "Air Roast" mode by rotating the dial.
4. Press the TEMP button and change the value to 400 degrees F.
5. Press the TIME button and change the value to 20 minutes, then press START to begin cooking.
6. After 10 minutes of cooking, add broccoli then return the pan to the Ninja Foodi digital Air Fryer oven.
7. Resume cooking for another 10 minutes.
8. Garnish with sesame seeds.
9. Serve warm.

Serving Suggestion: Serve the chicken fry inside warmed pita bread.

Variation Tip: Add canned corns to the stir fry.

Nutritional Information Per Serving:
Calories 388 | Fat 8g |Sodium 339mg | Carbs 8g | Fiber 1g | Sugar 2g | Protein 13g

Honey Lime Chicken Wings

Prep Time: 15 minutes.

Cook Time: 25 minutes.

Serves: 4

Ingredients:

- 3 tablespoons sriracha sauce
- ¼ cup honey
- 2 tablespoons soy sauce
- 1 tablespoon brown sugar
- 1 tablespoon ground ginger
- Zest and juice of 2 limes
- 2 ½ lbs. chicken wings

Preparation:

1. Whisk sriracha sauce, honey, soy sauce, brown sugar, ginger, lime zest, and lime juice in a bowl.
2. Add the chicken to the bowl and mix well to coat.
3. Cover the chicken and refrigerate for 1 hour or more to marinate.
4. Place the chicken wings in the Ninja Air Fryer basket and spray them with cooking spray.
5. Transfer the basket to the Ninja Foodi Digital Air Fryer Oven and close the door.
6. Select "Air Crisp" mode by rotating the dial.
7. Press the TEMP button and change the value to 400 degrees F.
8. Press the TIME button and change the value to 25 minutes, then press START to begin cooking.
9. Toss the chicken wings once cooked halfway through, then resume cooking.
10. Serve warm.

Serving Suggestion: Serve the chicken wings with steaming white rice.

Variation Tip: Add 1 tbsp tahini to the seasoning and marinate.

Nutritional Information Per Serving:

Calories 301 | Fat 16g | Sodium 189mg | Carbs 32g | Fiber 0.3g | Sugar 0.1g | Protein 28.2g

Chicken Tenders

Prep Time: 15 minutes.
Cook Time: 13 minutes.
Serves: 4

Ingredients:

- 1 lb. chicken tenderloins
- ½ cup flour
- 2 eggs, beaten
- ⅓ cup Italian breadcrumbs
- ⅓ cup Parmesan cheese, grated
- ½ teaspoons garlic salt
- ½ teaspoons black pepper
- olive oil spray

Preparation:

1. Spread the flour in a bowl, mix breadcrumbs with parmesan cheese, garlic salt, and black pepper in another bowl.
2. Beat eggs with black pepper and salt in a third bowl.
3. Coat the chicken tenders with the flour, then dip them in the eggs and coat them with breadcrumbs mixture.
4. Place the chicken tenders in the Ninja Air Fryer basket and spray them with cooking spray.
5. Transfer the basket to the Ninja Foodi Digital Air Fryer Oven and close the door.
6. Select "Air Crisp" mode by rotating the dial.
7. Press the TEMP button and change the value to 400 degrees F.
8. Press the TIME button and change the value to 13 minutes, then press START to begin cooking.
9. Toss the coated chicken tenders once cooked halfway through and resume cooking.
10. Serve warm.

Serving Suggestion: Serve the chicken tenders with chili garlic sauce.

Variation Tip: Add dried herbs to the flour for seasoning.

Nutritional Information Per Serving:
Calories 231 | Fat 20g | Sodium 941mg | Carbs 30g | Fiber 0.9g | Sugar 1.4g | Protein 14.6g

Chicken, Sweet Potatoes and Broccoli

Prep Time: 15 minutes.
Cook Time: 22 minutes.
Serves: 4

Ingredients:

- 3 tablespoons olive oil
- 1 tablespoon Cajun seasoning
- 1 head broccoli, cut into florets
- 1 teaspoon salt
- 1 lb. boneless chicken breasts, cut into cubes
- 2 medium sweet potatoes, peeled, cut into cubes
- 1 teaspoon ground black pepper

Preparation:

1. Toss chicken, broccoli and sweet potatoes with Cajun seasoning and 1 tablespoon oil in the Ninja sheet pan.
2. Transfer the sheet pan to the Ninja Foodi Digital Air Fryer Oven and close the door.
3. Select "Air Roast" mode by rotating the dial.
4. Press the TEMP button and change the value to 415 degrees F.
5. Press the TIME button and change the value to 22 minutes, then press START to begin cooking.
6. Serve warm.

Serving Suggestion: Serve the chicken broccoli with a fresh crouton's salad.

Variation Tip: Add a drizzle of cheese on top.

Nutritional Information Per Serving:

Calories 440 | Fat 7.9g | Sodium 581mg | Carbs 21.8g | Fiber 2.6g | Sugar 7g | Protein 37.2g

Chicken Sheet Pan Meal

Prep Time: 15 minutes.
Cook Time: 35 minutes.
Serves: 4

Ingredients:

- ¼ cup olive oil
- 1 teaspoon sea salt
- ½ teaspoons black pepper
- 12 oz. red potatoes, diced
- 2 medium zucchinis, diced
- 1 medium yellow squash, diced
- 1 red onion, diced
- 1 bulb garlic, peeled and minced
- 16 oz. chicken breast, diced
- 8 sprigs rosemary fresh
- 3 lemons, sliced

Preparation:

1. Toss chicken with olive oil, salt, black pepper, garlic, rosemary, squash, and zucchini in a large bowl.
2. Spread the potatoes in the Ninja sheet pan.
3. Transfer the sheet pan to the Ninja Foodi Digital Air Fryer Oven and close the door.
4. Select "Air Roast" mode by rotating the dial.
5. Press the TEMP button and change the value to 450 degrees F.
6. Press the TIME button and change the value to 10 minutes, then press START to begin cooking.
7. Add chicken, zucchini, onion, garlic, and squash to the sheet pan.
8. Drizzle black pepper, salt, and oil over the chicken and veggies.
9. Return the sheet pan to the Ninja Digital Air Fryer oven.
10. Select "Air Crisp" mode by rotating the dial.
11. Press the TEMP button and change the value to 325 degrees F.
12. Press the TIME button and change the value to 25 minutes, then press START to begin cooking.
13. Serve warm.

Serving Suggestion: Serve the sheet pan meal with tomato sauce and toasted bread slices.

Variation Tip: Add butter sauce on top of the veggies before cooking.

Nutritional Information Per Serving:

Calories 419 | Fat 13g | Sodium 432mg | Carbs 9.1g | Fiber 3g | Sugar 1g | Protein 33g

Turkey Ham Casserole

Prep Time: 15 minutes.

Cook Time: 35 minutes.

Serves: 8

Ingredients:

- 1 2/3 oz. butter
- 3 leeks, sliced
- 1 oz. plain flour
- ½ cup white wine
- 2 cups chicken stock
- ½ cup double cream
- 1 lb. cooked turkey, diced
- 5 oz. ham, diced
- 2 tarragon sprigs, leaves finely chopped
- 3 ½ oz. peas, defrosted
- 6 cubes of frozen spinach, defrosted
- Salt and black pepper, to taste

Crust:

- 3 ½ oz. breadcrumbs
- 1 small onion, grated
- 3 ½ oz. chestnuts, grated
- 1 oz. dried cranberries, soaked in warm water (optional)
- 2 teaspoons dried sage
- Small bunch of parsley, finely chopped
- 1 large knob of butter

Preparation:

1. Sauté butter with leeks and seasoning in a skillet until soft.
2. Stir in flour and mix well. Pour in stock and cream, then mix well.
3. Add ham, turkey, tarragon, and peas, then mix until sauce until its sauce thickens.
4. Add spinach, black pepper, and salt, then mix well.
5. Spread this leek mixture in a casserole dish and top it with breadcrumbs, chestnuts, herbs, cranberries, and onion.
6. Add butter, black pepper, and salt on top of the casserole.
7. Transfer the casserole dish to the Ninja Foodi Digital Air Fryer Oven and close the door.
8. Select the "Bake" mode by rotating the dial.

9. Press the TEMP button and change the value to 350 degrees F.
10. Press the TIME button and change the value to 30 minutes, then press START to begin cooking.
11. Serve warm.

Serving Suggestion: Serve the casserole with roasted veggies on the side.

Variation Tip: Add peas and corn to the casserole.

Nutritional Information Per Serving:

Calories 334 | Fat 16g | Sodium 462mg | Carbs 31g | Fiber 0.4g | Sugar 3g | Protein 35.3g

Chapter 4: Beef, Pork, and Lamb Recipes

Italian Pasta Bake

Prep Time: 15 minutes.
Cook Time: 57 minutes.
Serves: 6

Ingredients:

- 2 lbs. ground beef
- 1 large onion, chopped
- 2 garlic cloves, minced
- 1 can (14 ½ oz.) tomatoes, diced, undrained
- 1 teaspoon Italian seasoning
- 3 cups pasta shells
- 1 jar (24 oz.) spaghetti sauce
- 3 plum tomatoes, sliced
- 3/4 cup provolone cheese, shredded
- 1 can (4 oz.) mushroom, drained
- 3/4 cup mozzarella cheese, shredded

Preparation:

1. Sauté beef and onion with oil in a skillet for 6 minutes.
2. Stir in garlic and cook for 1 minute.
3. Add Italian seasoning, mushrooms, tomatoes, and spaghetti sauce.
4. Boil and then cook on a simmer for 20 minutes.
5. Meanwhile, boil pasta in a cooking pot according to the instructions.
6. Drain and add pasta to the beef sauce.
7. Spread the beef- pasta in a casserole dish, then add cheese on top.
8. Transfer the sheet pan to the Ninja Foodi Digital Air Fryer Oven and close the door.
9. Select the "Bake" mode by rotating the dial.
10. Press the TEMP button and change the value to 350 degrees F.
11. Press the TIME button and change the value to 30 minutes, then press START to begin cooking.
12. Slice and serve warm.

Serving Suggestion: Serve the casserole with mashed potatoes.

Variation Tip: Use chicken mince instead of beef.

Nutritional Information Per Serving:
Calories 305 | Fat 25g |Sodium 532mg | Carbs 2.3g | Fiber 0.4g | Sugar 2g | Protein 18.3g

Sausage Casserole

Prep Time: 15 minutes.

Cook Time: 55 minutes.

Serves: 8

Ingredients:

- 1 lb. ground pork sausage
- 1 teaspoon mustard powder
- ½ teaspoon salt
- 4 eggs, beaten
- 2 cups of milk
- 6 white bread slices, toasted and cubed
- 8 oz. Cheddar cheese, shredded

Preparation:

1. Sauté sausage in a skillet until brown then keep it aside.
2. Whisk salt, eggs, milk, and mustard powder in a bowl.
3. Spread the bread cubes, sausage in a casserole dish.
4. Pour this mixture on top and drizzle cheese.
5. Cover it with a foil sheet and refrigerate the sausage casserole for 1 hour.
6. Transfer the casserole dish to the Ninja Foodi Digital Air Fryer Oven and close the door.
7. Select the "Bake" mode by rotating the dial.
8. Press the TEMP button and change the value to 350 degrees F.
9. Press the TIME button and change the value to 45 minutes, then press START to begin cooking.
10. Remove the foil and continue baking for another 10 minutes.
11. Serve warm.

Serving Suggestion: Serve the casserole with toasted bread slices.

Variation Tip: Add crumbled bacon on top.

Nutritional Information Per Serving:

Calories 325 | Fat 16g | Sodium 431mg | Carbs 22g | Fiber 1.2g | Sugar 4g | Protein 23g

Christmas Casserole

Prep Time: 15 minutes.

Cook Time: 30 minutes.

Serves: 8

Ingredients:

- 7 eggs
- 1/4 cup milk
- 1 (16 oz.) package biscuit dough, diced
- 1 ½ cups cheddar cheese, shredded
- 4 green onions, chopped
- 8 slices bacon, cooked and chopped

Preparation:

1. Beat eggs with milk in a casserole dish.
2. Add onions, cheese, biscuit pieces, and bacon.
3. Transfer the casserole dish to the Ninja Foodi Digital Air Fryer Oven and close the door.
4. Select the "Bake" mode by rotating the dial.
5. Press the TEMP button and change the value to 350 degrees F.
6. Press the TIME button and change the value to 30 minutes, then press START to begin cooking.
7. Serve warm.

Serving Suggestion: Serve this casserole with pasta or spaghetti.

Variation Tip: Add toasted croutons on top.

Nutritional Information Per Serving:

Calories 425 | Fat 14g | Sodium 411mg | Carbs 44g | Fiber 0.3g | Sugar 1g | Protein 8.3g

Holiday Ham

Prep Time: 15 minutes.
Cook Time: 30 minutes.
Serves: 6

Ingredients:

- 3 lbs. boneless spiral ham

Glaze

- ½ cup honey
- ¼ cup brown sugar
- 2 tablespoons Dijon mustard
- ¼ teaspoons nutmeg
- 1/4 teaspoon cayenne pepper
- ¼ teaspoons salt

Preparation:

1. Wrap the ham in a foil sheet and place it in the Ninja sheet pan.
2. Transfer the sheet pan to the Ninja Foodi Digital Air Fryer Oven and close the door.
3. Select "Air Roast" mode by rotating the dial.
4. Press the TEMP button and change the value to 300 degrees F.
5. Press the TIME button and change the value to 15 minutes, then press START to begin cooking.
6. Mix remaining ingredients for glaze in a saucepan and cook it to a boil with occasional stirring.
7. Unwrap the ham and brush it with the prepared glazed.
8. Return the ham to the Ninja digital Air Fryer oven.
9. Continue roasting the ham for another 15 minutes at 350 degrees F.
10. Slice and serve warm.

Serving Suggestion: Serve the ham with sweet potato casserole.

Variation Tip: Add cheese on top of the ham and then broil after cooking.

Nutritional Information Per Serving:

Calories 425 | Fat 15g | Sodium 345mg | Carbs 12.3g | Fiber 1.4g | Sugar 3g | Protein 23.3g

Pork Meatballs

Prep Time: 15 minutes.
Cook Time: 11 minutes.
Serves: 6

Ingredients:

- 1 ½ lbs. ground pork
- 1 cup plain bread crumbs
- ½ cup milk
- 1 large egg
- ½ cup celery, chopped
- ¼ cup onion, chopped
- 2 tablespoons sage, chopped
- 1 tablespoon rosemary, chopped
- 1 tablespoon thyme leaves
- 1 tablespoon parsley, chopped
- ½ teaspoon salt
- ⅛ teaspoon black pepper

Preparation:

1. Soak breadcrumbs in milk in a large bowl and keep it aside for 5 minutes.
2. Stir in ground pork, egg, celery, onion, sage, rosemary, thyme leaves, parsley, black pepper, and salt.
3. Mix well and make golf-ball sized meatballs out of this mixture.
4. Place the meatballs in the Ninja Air Fryer basket and spray them with cooking spray.
5. Transfer the basket to the Ninja Foodi Digital Air Fryer Oven and close the door.
6. Select "Air Crispy" mode by rotating the dial.
7. Press the TEMP button and change the value to 390 degrees F.
8. Press the TIME button and change the value to 11 minutes, then press START to begin cooking.
9. Toss the meatballs once cooked halfway through, then resume cooking.
10. Serve warm.

Serving Suggestion: Serve the meatballs with mashed potatoes.

Variation Tip: Roll the meatballs in breadcrumbs or crushed cornflakes before baking.

Nutritional Information Per Serving:

Calories 91 | Fat 5g | Sodium 88mg | Carbs 3g | Fiber 0g | Sugar 0g | Protein 7g

Cauliflower Pork Casserole

Prep Time: 15 minutes.
Cook Time: 30 minutes.
Serves: 8

Ingredients:

- 3 (16 oz.) packages frozen cauliflower
- 2 cups sour cream
- 2 cups cheddar cheese, shredded
- 3 teaspoons chicken bouillon granules
- 1 ½ teaspoon ground mustard
- 1/4 cup butter, cubed
- 1 cup pork, minced
- 3/4 cup California walnuts, chopped

Preparation:

1. Boil the cauliflowers in hot water until soft. Drain and transfer the cauliflower to a 13x9 inches casserole dish.
2. Sauté butter with walnuts and pork in a skillet until golden brown.
3. Spread this mixture on top of the cauliflower.
4. Beat sour cream, bouillon, mustard, and cheese in a bowl.
5. Spoon this mixture on top of the cauliflower pork casserole.
6. Transfer the casserole dish to the Ninja Foodi Digital Air Fryer Oven and close the door.
7. Select the "Bake" mode by rotating the dial.
8. Press the TEMP button and change the value to 350 degrees F.
9. Press the TIME button and change the value to 20 minutes, then press START to begin cooking.
10. Serve warm.

Serving Suggestion: Serve the casserole with crispy bacon on top.

Variation Tip: Add a layer of the boiled pasta to the casserole.

Nutritional Information Per Serving:
Calories 276 | Fat 21g | Sodium 476mg | Carbs 12g | Fiber 3g | Sugar 4g | Protein 10g

Balsamic Pork Veggie Meal

Prep Time: 15 minutes.
Cook Time: 30 minutes.
Serves: 4

Ingredients:

- 4 boneless pork chops
- 1 green bell pepper, chopped
- 1 orange bell pepper, chopped
- 8 baby Yukon gold potatoes, chopped
- 1 tablespoon rosemary, minced
- ¼ cup balsamic vinegar
- 1 tablespoon honey
- 2 teaspoons garlic powder
- Salt and black pepper to taste

Preparation:

1. Mix the pork chops with bell pepper, gold potatoes, rosemary, balsamic vinegar, honey, garlic powder, black pepper and salt in the Ninja sheet pan.
2. Transfer the sheet pan to the Ninja Foodi Digital Air Fryer Oven and close the door.
3. Select the "Bake" mode by rotating the dial.
4. Press the TEMP button and change the value to 325 degrees F.
5. Press the TIME button and change the value to 30 minutes, then press START to begin cooking.
6. Serve warm.

Serving Suggestion: Serve the pork meal with fresh greens salad.

Variation Tip: Wrap the pork chops, spices, and vegetables in a foil sheet before baking for a rich taste.

Nutritional Information Per Serving:

Calories 380 | Fat 20g | Sodium 686mg | Carbs 33g | Fiber 1g | Sugar 1.2g | Protein 21g

Sheet Pan Pork with Apples

Prep Time: 15 minutes.
Cook Time: 23 minutes.
Serves: 4

Ingredients:

- 1 medium sweet potato, sliced
- 2 (6 oz.) pork chops
- 1 small apple, sliced
- 6 oz. asparagus
- 2 tablespoons olive oil

- 2 teaspoons bourbon BBQ sauce

Spice Blend

- ½ teaspoons fine grind sea salt
- ½ teaspoons black pepper
- ½ teaspoons cinnamon
- ½ teaspoons chipotle powder

Preparation:

1. Mix spice blend ingredients in a small bowl.
2. Toss sweet potatoes with olive oil and 1/3 spice blend in the Ninja sheet pan.
3. Transfer the sheet pan to the Ninja Foodi Digital Air Fryer Oven and close the door.
4. Select "Air Roast" mode by rotating the dial.
5. Press the TEMP button and change the value to 350 degrees F.
6. Press the TIME button and change the value to 15 minutes, then press START to begin cooking.
7. After 10 minutes, press PAUSE and add asparagus to the sweet potatoes.
8. Drizzle black pepper, oil, and salt over the asparagus and resume cooking.
9. Season pork and apples with the spice blend and BBQ sauce on a bowl.
10. Add the apples and pork to the sweet potatoes in the sheet pan.
11. Transfer the sheet pans to the Ninja Foodi Digital Air Fryer Oven and close the door.
12. Select "Air Crisp" mode by rotating the dial.
13. Press the TEMP button and change the value to 325 degrees F.
14. Press the TIME button and change the value to 8 minutes, then press START to begin cooking.
15. Serve warm.

Serving Suggestion: Serve the pork with boiled rice or spaghetti.

Variation Tip: Use apple sauce for seasoning.

Nutritional Information Per Serving:

Calories 361 | Fat 16g | Sodium 515mg | Carbs 19.3g | Fiber 0.1g | Sugar 18.2g | Protein 33.3g

Lamb Sirloin Steak

Prep Time: 15 minutes.
Cook Time: 15 minutes.
Serves: 2

Ingredients:

- 1/2 onion, chopped
- 4 ginger slices
- 5 garlic cloves, minced
- 1 teaspoon garam masala
- 1 teaspoon ground fennel
- 1 teaspoon ground cinnamon
- 1/2 teaspoon ground cardamom
- 1 teaspoon cayenne pepper
- 1 teaspoon salt
- 1 lb. boneless lamb sirloin steaks

Preparation:

1. Blend ginger, garlic, onion, garam masala, fennel, cinnamon, cardamom, cayenne pepper, and salt in a blender.
2. Place the lamb chops in the Ninja sheet pan and rub the spice blend on both sides.
3. Transfer the sheet pan to the Ninja Foodi Digital Air Fryer Oven and close the door.
4. Select "Air Crisp" mode by rotating the dial.
5. Press the TEMP button and change the value to 330 degrees F.
6. Press the TIME button and change the value to 15 minutes, then press START to begin cooking.
7. Flip the lamb once cooked halfway through, then resume cooking.
8. Serve warm.

Serving Suggestion: Serve the lamb with garlic slices and fresh herbs on top.

Variation Tip: Add butter to the chops before cooking.

Nutritional Information Per Serving:

Calories 405 | Fat 22.7g |Sodium 227mg | Carbs 26.1g | Fiber 1.4g | Sugar 0.9g | Protein 45.2g

Masala Chops

Prep Time: 15 minutes.
Cook Time: 15 minutes.
Serves: 2

Ingredients:

- 1 lb. Lamb chops
- 1 ½ tablespoons red chili powder
- 1 tablespoon turmeric powder
- 1/2 tablespoons garam masala powder
- 1 teaspoon salt
- 1 tablespoon cumin powder
- 1 tablespoon white vinegar
- 2 tablespoons ginger garlic paste
- 3 tablespoons vegetable oil

Preparation:

1. Place the lamb chops in the Ninja Sheet pan.
2. Sauté ginger garlic paste with oil in a skillet until golden.
3. Add rest of the spices, then mix well, then allow it cool.
4. Pour this mixture over the lamb chops and rub it on both sides.
5. Transfer the sheet pan to the Ninja Foodi Digital Air Fryer Oven and close the door.
6. Select "Air Roast" mode by rotating the dial.
7. Press the TEMP button and change the value to 390 degrees F.
8. Press the TIME button and change the value to 10 minutes, then press START to begin cooking.
9. Serve warm.

Serving Suggestion: Serve the chops with boiled peas, carrots, and potatoes on the side.

Variation Tip: Mix the spices with yogurt and marinate the chops in this mixture for 1 hour then bake.

Nutritional Information Per Serving:
Calories 345 | Fat 36g |Sodium 272mg | Carbs 41g | Fiber 0.2g | Sugar 0.1g | Protein 22.5g

Lamb Chops with Garlic Sauce

Prep Time: 15 minutes.

Cook Time: 22 minutes.

Serves: 8

Ingredients:

- 1 garlic bulb
- 3 tablespoons olive oil
- 1 tablespoon oregano, chopped
- Sea salt, to taste
- Black pepper, to taste
- 8 lamb chops

Preparation:

1. Rub the garlic and olive oil over the chops and place them in the Ninja Air Fryer basket.
2. Transfer the basket to the Ninja Foodi Digital Air Fryer Oven and close the door.
3. Select "Air Roast" mode by rotating the dial.
4. Press the TEMP button and change the value to 390 degrees F.
5. Press the TIME button and change the value to 12 minutes, then press START to begin cooking.
6. Transfer the garlic to a bowl and allow it to cool.
7. Mix herbs with olive oil, black pepper and salt in a bowl.
8. Rub this mixture over the lamb chops and marinate for 5 minutes.
9. Squeeze the garlic out of its peel and rub it over the chops.
10. Place the chops in the sheet pan.
11. Transfer the sheet pan to the Ninja Foodi Digital Air Fryer Oven and close the door.
12. Select "Air Crisp" mode by rotating the dial.
13. Press the TEMP button and change the value to 350 degrees F.
14. Press the TIME button and change the value to 10 minutes, then press START to begin cooking.
15. Flip the chops once cooked halfway through and resume cooking.
16. Serve warm.

Serving Suggestion: Serve the chops with sautéed green beans and mashed potatoes.

Variation Tip: Drizzle parmesan cheese on top before cooking.

Nutritional Information Per Serving:

Calories 395 | Fat 9.5g |Sodium 655mg | Carbs 13.4g | Fiber 0.4g | Sugar 0.4g | Protein 28.3g

Herbed Lamb Chops

Prep Time: 15 minutes.
Cook Time: 17 minutes.
Serves: 2

Ingredients:

- 1 teaspoon rosemary
- 1 teaspoon thyme
- 1 teaspoon oregano
- 1 teaspoon salt
- 1 teaspoon coriander
- 2 tablespoons olive oil
- 2 tablespoons lemon juice
- 1 lb. lamb chops

Preparation:

1. Mix lemon juice, rosemary, thyme, oregano, salt, and coriander in a bowl.
2. Rub this mixture over the lamb chops and marinate for 10 minutes.
3. Place the lamb chops in the Ninja sheet pan.
4. Transfer the sheet pan to the Ninja Foodi Digital Air Fryer Oven and close the door.
5. Select "Air Roast" mode by rotating the dial.
6. Press the TEMP button and change the value to 390 degrees F.
7. Press the TIME button and change the value to 7 minutes, then press START to begin cooking.
8. Flip the chops once cooked halfway through, then resume cooking.
9. Serve warm.

Serving Suggestion: Serve the chops with fresh green and mashed potatoes.

Variation Tip: Add sweet potatoes or squash instead on the side of the chops before roasting.

Nutritional Information Per Serving:

Calories 301 | Fat 5g |Sodium 340mg | Carbs 24.7g | Fiber 1.2g | Sugar 1.3g | Protein 15.3g

Steak Bites Mushrooms

Prep Time: 15 minutes.

Cook Time: 15 minutes.

Serves: 2

Ingredients:

- 1 lb. steaks, cut into cubes
- 8 oz. mushrooms, halved
- 2 tablespoons butter, melted
- 1 teaspoon Worcestershire sauce
- ½ teaspoon garlic powder
- Salt, to taste
- Black pepper, to taste
- Chili flakes, for finishing

Preparation:

1. Toss steak cubes with mushrooms in a bowl.
2. Mix melted butter with garlic powder, black pepper, and Worcestershire sauce in a small bowl.
3. Spread the mushrooms and steak in the Ninja sheet pan.
4. Transfer the sheet pan to the Ninja Foodi Digital Air Fryer Oven and close the door.
5. Select "Air Roast" mode by rotating the dial.
6. Press the TEMP button and change the value to 400 degrees F.
7. Press the TIME button and change the value to 15 minutes, then press START to begin cooking.
8. Toss the steaks once cooked halfway through, then resume cooking.
9. Garnish with chili flakes, black pepper and salt.
10. Serve warm.

Serving Suggestion: Serve the steak and mushrooms with quinoa salad.

Variation Tip: Add barbecue sauce to the beef and mushrooms.

Nutritional Information Per Serving:

Calories 448 | Fat 23g | Sodium 350mg | Carbs 18g | Fiber 6.3g | Sugar 1g | Protein 40.3g

Glazed Steaks

Prep Time: 15 minutes.
Cook Time: 15 minutes.
Serves: 2

Ingredients:

- 2 (6 oz.) sirloin steaks
- 2 tablespoons soy sauce
- 1/2 tablespoons Worcestershire sauce
- 2 tablespoons brown sugar
- 1 tablespoon ginger, peeled and grated
- 1 tablespoon garlic, crushed
- 1 teaspoon seasoned salt
- Salt and black pepper, to taste

Preparation:

1. Mix soy sauce, Worcestershire sauce, brown sugar, ginger, salt and black pepper in a sealable bag.
2. Add steak to the spice blend and seal the bag.
3. Shake it well and marinate for 8 hours in the refrigerator.
4. Spread the steaks in the Ninja sheet pan.
5. Transfer the sheet pan to the Ninja Foodi Digital Air Fryer Oven and close the door.
6. Select "Air Roast" mode by rotating the dial.
7. Press the TEMP button and change the value to 400 degrees F.
8. Press the TIME button and change the value to 15 minutes, then press START to begin cooking.
9. Serve warm.

Serving Suggestion: Serve the beef steak with sautéed vegetables and toasted bread slices.

Variation Tip: Use honey instead of sugar for a mild sweet taste.

Nutritional Information Per Serving:
Calories 309 | Fat 25g |Sodium 463mg | Carbs 9.9g | Fiber 0.3g | Sugar 0.3g | Protein 18g

Bacon Meatloaf

Prep Time: 15 minutes.
Cook Time: 40 minutes.
Serves: 6

Ingredients:

- ½ lb. thick cut bacon
- ½ lb. ground beef
- ½ lb. ground pork
- 1 cup almond flour
- ½ yellow onion, diced
- 1 red bell pepper, diced
- 2 tablespoons ketchup
- 1 tablespoon spicy brown mustard
- 1 teaspoon salt

- 1 teaspoon garlic powder
- 1/2 teaspoon white pepper
- 1/2 teaspoon celery salt
- 1/4 teaspoon cayenne pepper
- 1 egg

Sauce:

- 1/2 cup ketchup
- 3 tablespoons maple syrup

Preparation:

1. Mix beef, pork, almond flour, and the rest of the meatloaf ingredients in a large bowl except bacon.
2. Spread the meatloaf mixture in a greased 9x5 inches meatloaf pan, then cover it with bacon slices.
3. Transfer the meatloaf pan to the Ninja Foodi Digital Air Fryer Oven and close the door.
4. Select "Air Roast" mode by rotating the dial.
5. Press the TEMP button and change the value to 350 degrees F.
6. Press the TIME button and change the value to 30 minutes, then press START to begin cooking.
7. Mix ketchup with maple syrup in a bowl.
8. Brush it with maple syrup and return it to the Ninja Digital Air Fryer oven.
9. Cook this meatloaf for another 10 minutes.
10. Slice and serve warm.

Serving Suggestion: Serve the meatloaf with mashed potatoes.

Variation Tip: Roast the meatloaf without bacon slices directly in a meatloaf pan.

Nutritional Information Per Serving:
Calories 537 | Fat 20g | Sodium 719mg | Carbs 25.1g | Fiber 0.9g | Sugar 1.4g | Protein 37.8g

Chapter 5: Fish & Seafood Recipes

Buttered Salmon

Preparation Time: 10 minutes
Cooking Time: 10 minutes
Servings: 2

Ingredients:

- 2 (6-ounce) salmon fillets
- Salt and freshly ground black pepper, to taste
- 1 tablespoon butter, melted

Preparation:

1. Season each salmon fillet with salt and black pepper and then, coat with the butter.
2. Press "Power Button" of Ninja Foodi Digital Air Fry Oven and turn the dial to select "Air Fry" mode.
3. Press "Time Button" and again turn the dial to set the cooking time to 10 minutes.
4. Now push "Temp Button" and rotate the dial to set the temperature at 360 degrees F.
5. Press "Start/Pause" button to start.
6. When the unit beeps to show that it is preheated, open the lid and grease the air fry basket.
7. Arrange the salmon fillets into the prepared air fry basket and insert in the oven.
8. When cooking time is complete, open the lid and transfer the salmon fillets onto serving plates.
9. Serve hot.

Serving Suggestions: Enjoy with roasted parsnip puree.

Variation Tip: Salmon should look bright and shiny.

Nutritional Information per Serving:

Calories: 276|**Fat:** 16.3g|**Sat Fat:** 5.2g|**Carbohydrates:** 0g|**Fiber:** 0g|**Sugar:** 0g|**Protein:** 33.1g

Herbed Salmon

Preparation Time: 10 minutes
Cooking Time: 10 minutes
Servings: 2

Ingredients:

- 1 tablespoon fresh lime juice
- ½ tablespoons olive oil
- Salt and freshly ground black pepper, to taste
- 1 garlic clove, minced
- ½ teaspoon fresh thyme leaves, chopped
- ½ teaspoon fresh rosemary, chopped
- 2 (7-ounce) salmon fillets

Preparation:

1. In a bowl, add all the ingredients except the salmon and mix well.
2. Add the salmon fillets and coat with the mixture generously.
3. Press "Power Button" of Ninja Foodi Digital Air Fry Oven and turn the dial to select "Air Bake" mode.
4. Press "Time Button" and again turn the dial to set the cooking time to 10 minutes.
5. Now push "Temp Button" and rotate the dial to set the temperature at 400 degrees F.
6. Press "Start/Pause" button to start.
7. When the unit beeps to show that it is preheated, open the lid.
8. Arrange the salmon fillets over the greased wire rack and insert in the oven.
9. Flip the fillets once halfway through.
10. When cooking time is complete, open the lid and transfer the salmon fillets onto serving plates.
11. Serve hot.

Serving Suggestions: Serve with steamed asparagus.

Variation Tip: For best result, use freshly squeezed lime juice.

Nutritional Information per Serving:

Calories: 297|**Fat:** 15.8g|**Sat Fat:** 2.3g|**Carbohydrates:** 0.9g|**Fiber:** 0.3g|**Sugar:** 0g|**Protein:** 38.6g

Glazed Salmon

Preparation Time: 10 minutes
Cooking Time: 8 minutes
Servings: 2

Ingredients:

- 2 (6-ounce) salmon fillets
- Salt, to taste
- 2 tablespoons honey

Preparation:

1. Sprinkle the salmon fillets with salt and then coat with honey.
2. Press "Power Button" of Ninja Foodi Digital Air Fry Oven and turn the dial to select "Air Fry" mode.
3. Press "Time Button" and again turn the dial to set the cooking time to 8 minutes.
4. Now push "Temp Button" and rotate the dial to set the temperature at 355 degrees F.
5. Press "Start/Pause" button to start.
6. When the unit beeps to show that it is preheated, open the lid and grease the air fry basket.
7. Arrange the salmon fillets into the prepared air fry basket and insert in the oven.
8. When cooking time is complete, open the lid and transfer the salmon fillets onto serving plates.
9. Serve hot.

Serving Suggestions: Fresh baby greens will be great if served with glazed salmon.

Variation Tip: honey can be replaced with maple syrup too.

Nutritional Information per Serving:

Calories: 289|**Fat:** 10.5g|**Sat Fat:** 1.5g|**Carbohydrates:** 17.3g|**Fiber:** 0g|**Sugar:** 17.3g|**Protein:** 33.1g

Ranch Tilapia

Preparation Time: 15 minutes
Cooking Time: 13 minutes
Servings: 4

Ingredients:

- ¾ cup cornflakes, crushed
- 1 (1-ounce) packet dry ranch-style dressing mix
- 2½ tablespoons vegetable oil
- 2 eggs
- 4 (6-ounce) tilapia fillets

Preparation:

1. In a shallow bowl, crack the eggs and beat slightly.
2. In another bowl, add the cornflakes, ranch dressing, and oil and mix until a crumbly mixture forms.
3. Dip the fish fillets into egg and then, coat with the breadcrumbs mixture.
4. Press "Power Button" of Ninja Foodi Digital Air Fry Oven and turn the dial to select "Air Fry" mode.
5. Press "Time Button" and again turn the dial to set the cooking time to 13 minutes.
6. Now push "Temp Button" and rotate the dial to set the temperature at 356 degrees F.
7. Press "Start/Pause" button to start.
8. When the unit beeps to show that it is preheated, open the lid and grease the air fry basket.
9. Arrange the tilapia fillets into the prepared air fry basket and insert in the oven. When cooking time is complete, open the lid and transfer the fillets onto serving plates.
10. Serve hot.

Serving Suggestions: Serve tilapia with lemon butter.

Variation Tip: The skin should be removed, either before cooking or before serving.

Nutritional Information per Serving:

Calories: 267|**Fat:** 12.2g|**Sat Fat:** 3g|**Carbohydrates:** 5.1g|**Fiber:** 0.2g|**Sugar:** 0.9g|**Protein:** 34.9g

Seasoned Catfish

Preparation Time: 15 minutes
Cooking Time: 23 minutes
Servings: 4

Ingredients:

- 4 (4-ounce) catfish fillets
- 2 tablespoons Italian seasoning
- Salt and freshly ground black pepper, to taste
- 1 tablespoon olive oil
- 1 tablespoon fresh parsley, chopped

Preparation:

1. Rub the fish fillets with seasoning, salt and black pepper generously and then coat with oil.
2. Press "Power Button" of Ninja Foodi Digital Air Fry Oven and turn the dial to select "Air Fry" mode.
3. Press "Time Button" and again turn the dial to set the cooking time to 20 minutes.
4. Now push "Temp Button" and rotate the dial to set the temperature at 400 degrees F.
5. Press "Start/Pause" button to start.
6. When the unit beeps to show that it is preheated, open the lid and grease the air fry basket.
7. Arrange the fish fillets into the prepared air fry basket and insert in the oven.
8. Flip the fish fillets once halfway through.
9. When cooking time is complete, open the lid and transfer the fillets onto serving plates.
10. Serve hot with the garnishing of parsley.

Serving Suggestions: Quinoa salad will be a great choice for serving.

Variation Tip: Season the fish according to your choice.

Nutritional Information per Serving:

Calories: 205|**Fat:** 14.2g|**Sat Fat:** 2.4g|**Carbohydrates:** 0.8g|**Fiber:** 0g|**Sugar:** 0.6g|**Protein:** 17.7g

Cod Parcel

Preparation Time: 15 minutes
Cooking Time: 15 minutes
Servings: 2

Ingredients:

- 2 tablespoons butter, melted
- 1 tablespoon fresh lemon juice
- ½ teaspoon dried tarragon
- Salt and freshly ground black pepper, to taste
- ½ cup red bell peppers, seeded and thinly sliced
- ½ cup carrots, peeled and julienned
- ½ cup fennel bulbs, julienned
- 2 (5-ounce) frozen cod fillets, thawed
- 1 tablespoon olive oil

Preparation:

1. In a large bowl, mix together the butter, lemon juice, tarragon, salt, and black pepper.
2. Add the bell pepper, carrot, and fennel bulb and generously coat with the mixture.
3. Arrange 2 large parchment squares onto a smooth surface.
4. Coat the cod fillets with oil and then sprinkle evenly with salt and black pepper.
5. Arrange 1 cod fillet onto each parchment square and top each evenly with the vegetables.
6. Top with any remaining sauce from the bowl.
7. Fold the parchment paper and crimp the sides to secure fish and vegetables.
8. Press "Power Button" of Ninja Foodi Digital Air Fry Oven and turn the dial to select "Air Fry" mode.
9. Press "Time Button" and again turn the dial to set the cooking time to 15 minutes.
10. Now push "Temp Button" and rotate the dial to set the temperature at 350 degrees F.
11. Press "Start/Pause" button to start.
12. When the unit beeps to show that it is preheated, open the lid.
13. Arrange the cod parcels into the air fry basket and insert in the oven.
14. When cooking time is complete, open the lid and transfer the cod parcels onto serving plates.
15. Carefully open the parcels and serve hot.

Serving Suggestions: Serve with the drizzling of lime juice.

Variation Tip: You can use veggies of your choice.

Nutritional Information per Serving:

Calories: 306|**Fat:** 20g|**Sat Fat:** 8.4g|**Carbohydrates:** 6.8g|**Fiber:** 1.8g|**Sugar:** 3g|**Protein:** 26.3g

Crusted Sole

Preparation Time: 15 minutes
Cooking Time: 15 minutes
Servings: 2

Ingredients:

- 2 teaspoons mayonnaise
- 1 teaspoon fresh chives, minced
- 3 tablespoons Parmesan cheese, shredded
- 2 tablespoons panko breadcrumbs
- Salt and freshly ground black pepper, to taste
- 2 (4-ounce) sole fillets

Preparation:

1. In a shallow dish, mix together the mayonnaise and chives.
2. In another shallow dish, mix together the cheese, breadcrumbs, salt and black pepper.
3. Coat the fish fillets with mayonnaise mixture and then roll in cheese mixture.
4. Arrange the sole fillets onto the greased sheet pan in a single layer.
5. Press "Power Button" of Ninja Foodi Digital Air Fry Oven and turn the dial to select "Air Bake" mode.
6. Press "Time Button" and again turn the dial to set the cooking time to 15 minutes.
7. Now push "Temp Button" and rotate the dial to set the temperature at 450 degrees F.
8. Press "Start/Pause" button to start.
9. When the unit beeps to show that it is preheated, open the lid and insert the sheet pan in the oven.
10. When cooking time is complete, open the lid and transfer the fish fillets onto serving plates.
11. Serve hot.

Serving Suggestions: Roasted potatoes make a great side for fish.

Variation Tip: If you want a gluten-free option then use pork rinds instead of breadcrumbs.

Nutritional Information per Serving:

Calories: 584|**Fat:** 14.6g|**Sat Fat:** 5.2g|**Carbohydrates:** 16.7g|**Fiber:** 0.4g|**Sugar:** 0.2g|**Protein:** 33.2g

Sweet & Tangy Herring

Preparation Time: 10 minutes
Cooking Time: 12 minutes
Servings: 2

Ingredients:

- 2 (5-ounce) herring fillets
- 1 garlic clove, minced
- 1 teaspoon fresh rosemary, minced
- 1 tablespoon butter, melted
- 1 tablespoon balsamic vinegar
- ¼ teaspoon maple syrup
- 1/8 teaspoon Sriracha

Preparation:

1. In a large resealable bag, place all the ingredients and seal the bag.
2. Shake the bag well to mix.
3. Place the bag in the refrigerator to marinate for at least 30 minutes.
4. Remove the fish fillets from bag and shake off the excess marinade.
5. Arrange the fish fillets onto the greased sheet pan in a single layer.
6. Press "Power Button" of Ninja Foodi Digital Air Fry Oven and turn the dial to select "Air Bake" mode.
7. Press "Time Button" and again turn the dial to set the cooking time to 12 minutes.
8. Now push "Temp Button" and rotate the dial to set the temperature at 450 degrees F.
9. Press "Start/Pause" button to start.
10. When the unit beeps to show that it is preheated, open the lid and insert the sheet pan in the oven.
11. Flip the fillets once halfway through.
12. When cooking time is complete, open the lid and transfer the fillets onto serving plates.
13. Serve hot.

Serving Suggestions: Enjoy with grilled vegetables.

Variation Tip: Use unsalted butter.

Nutritional Information per Serving:

Calories: 347|**Fat:** 22.3g|**Sat Fat:** 7.4g|**Carbohydrates:** 1.6g|**Fiber:** 0.3g|**Sugar:** 0.5g|**Protein:** 32.8g

Lemony Shrimp

Preparation Time: 15 minutes
Cooking Time: 8 minutes
Servings: 3

Ingredients:

- 2 tablespoons fresh lemon juice
- 1 tablespoon olive oil
- 1 teaspoon lemon pepper
- ¼ teaspoon paprika
- ¼ teaspoon garlic powder
- 12 ounces medium shrimp, peeled and deveined

Preparation:

1. In a large bowl, add all the ingredients except the shrimp and mix until well combined.
2. Add the shrimp and toss to coat well.
3. Arrange the shrimps onto a sheet pan.
4. Press "Power Button" of Ninja Foodi Digital Air Fry Oven and turn the dial to select "Air Fry" mode.
5. Press "Time Button" and again turn the dial to set the cooking time to 8 minutes.
6. Now push "Temp Button" and rotate the dial to set the temperature at 400 degrees F.
7. Press "Start/Pause" button to start.
8. When the unit beeps to show that it is preheated, open the lid and insert the sheet pan in the oven.
9. When cooking time is complete, open the lid and transfer the shrimp onto serving plates.
10. Serve hot.

Serving Suggestions: Serve with scalloped potatoes.

Variation Tip: Avoid shrimp that smell like ammonia.

Nutritional Information per Serving:

Calories: 164|**Fat:** 6.1g|**Sat Fat:** 0.8g|**Carbohydrates:** 0.9g|**Fiber:** 0.3g|**Sugar:** 0.3g|**Protein:** 24.5g

Halibut & Shrimp with Pasta

Preparation Time: 15 minutes
Cooking Time: 10 minutes
Servings: 4

Ingredients:

- 14 ounces pasta
- 4 tablespoons pesto, divided
- 4 (4-ounce) halibut steaks
- 2 tablespoons olive oil
- ½ pound tomatoes, chopped
- 8 large shrimp, peeled and deveined
- 2 tablespoons fresh lime juice
- 2 tablespoons fresh dill, chopped

Preparation:

1. In the bottom of a baking pan, spread 1 tablespoon of pesto.
2. Place halibut steaks and tomatoes over pesto in a single layer and drizzle with the oil.
3. Now, place the shrimp on top in a single layer.
4. Drizzle with lime juice and sprinkle with dill.
5. Press "Power Button" of Ninja Foodi Digital Air Fry Oven and turn the dial to select "Air Fry" mode.
6. Press "Time Button" and again turn the dial to set the cooking time to 8 minutes.
7. Now push "Temp Button" and rotate the dial to set the temperature at 390 degrees F.
8. Press "Start/Pause" button to start.
9. When the unit beeps to show that it is preheated, open the lid.
10. Place the pan over the wire rack and insert in the oven.
11. Meanwhile, in a large pan of salted boiling water, add the pasta and cook for about 8-10 minutes or until desired doneness.
12. Drain the pasta and transfer into a large bowl.
13. Add the remaining pesto and toss to coat well.
14. When cooking time is complete, open the lid and divide the pasta onto serving plates.
15. Top with the fish mixture and serve immediately.

Serving Suggestions: Serve with the topping of freshly grated Parmesan.

Variation Tip: Linguine pasta will be the best choice for this recipe.

Nutritional Information per Serving:

Calories: 606|**Fat:** 19.4g|**Sat Fat:** 3.2g|**Carbohydrates:** 59.1g|**Fiber:** 1.1g|**Sugar:** 2.5g|**Protein:** 47.4g

Herbed Scallops

Preparation Time: 15 minutes
Cooking Time: 14 minutes
Servings: 2

Ingredients:

- ¾ pound sea scallops, cleaned and pat dry
- 1 tablespoon butter, melted
- ¼ tablespoon fresh thyme, minced
- ¼ tablespoon fresh rosemary, minced
- Salt and freshly ground black pepper, to taste

Preparation:

1. In a large bowl, place the scallops, butter, herbs, salt, and black pepper and toss to coat well.
2. Press "Power Button" of Ninja Foodi Digital Air Fry Oven and turn the dial to select "Air Fry" mode.
3. Press "Time Button" and again turn the dial to set the cooking time to 4 minutes.
4. Now push "Temp Button" and rotate the dial to set the temperature at 390 degrees F.
5. Press "Start/Pause" button to start.
6. When the unit beeps to show that it is preheated, open the lid and grease the air fry basket.
7. Arrange the scallops into the air fry basket and insert in the oven.
8. When cooking time is complete, open the lid and transfer the scallops onto serving plates.
9. Serve hot.

Serving Suggestions: Potato fries will be great with these scallops.

Variation Tip: Remove the side muscles from the scallops.

Nutritional Information per Serving:

Calories: 203|**Fat:** 7.1g|**Sat Fat:** 3.8g|**Carbohydrates:** 4.5g|**Fiber:** 0.3g|**Sugar:** 0g|**Protein:** 28.7g

Prawn Burgers

Preparation Time: 15 minutes
Cooking Time: 6 minutes
Servings: 2

Ingredients:

- ½ cup prawns, peeled, deveined and chopped very finely
- ½ cup breadcrumbs
- 2-3 tablespoons onion, chopped finely
- ½ teaspoon fresh ginger, minced
- ½ teaspoon garlic, minced
- ½ teaspoon red chili powder
- ½ teaspoon ground cumin
- ¼ teaspoon ground turmeric
- Salt and freshly ground black pepper, to taste

Preparation:

1. In a bowl, add all ingredients and mix until well combined.
2. Make small sized patties from mixture.
3. Press "Power Button" of Ninja Foodi Digital Air Fry Oven and turn the dial to select "Air Fry" mode.
4. Press "Time Button" and again turn the dial to set the cooking time to 6 minutes.
5. Now push "Temp Button" and rotate the dial to set the temperature at 355 degrees F.
6. Press "Start/Pause" button to start.
7. When the unit beeps to show that it is preheated, open the lid and grease the air fry basket.
8. Arrange the patties into the prepared air fry basket and insert in the oven.
9. When cooking time is complete, open the lid and transfer the burgers onto serving plates.
10. Serve hot.

Serving Suggestions: Serve with tomato ketchup.

Variation Tip: Don't use frozen shrimp in this recipe.

Nutritional Information per Serving:

Calories: 186|**Fat:** 2.7g|**Sat Fat:** 0.7g|**Carbohydrates:** 22.5g|**Fiber:** 1.8g|**Sugar:** 2.2g|**Protein:** 16.9g

Chapter 6: Vegetable & Sides Recipes

Green Beans & Mushroom Casserole

Preparation Time: 15 minutes
Cooking Time: 12 minutes
Servings: 6

Ingredients:

- 24 ounces fresh green beans, trimmed
- 2 cups fresh button mushrooms, sliced
- 3 tablespoons olive oil
- 2 tablespoons fresh lemon juice
- 1 teaspoon ground sage
- 1 teaspoon garlic powder
- 1 teaspoon onion powder
- Salt and freshly ground black pepper, to taste
- 1/3 cup French fried onions

Preparation:

1. In a bowl, add the green beans, mushrooms, oil, lemon juice, sage, and spices and toss to coat well.
2. Press "Power Button" of Ninja Foodi Digital Air Fry Oven and turn the dial to select "Air Fry" mode.
3. Press "Time Button" and again turn the dial to set the cooking time to 12 minutes.
4. Now push "Temp Button" and rotate the dial to set the temperature at 400 degrees F.
5. Press "Start/Pause" button to start.
6. When the unit beeps to show that it is preheated, open the lid and grease the air fry basket.
7. Arrange the mushroom mixture into the prepared air fry basket and insert in the oven.
8. Shake the mushroom mixture occasionally.
9. When cooking time is complete, open the lid and transfer the mushroom mixture into a serving dish.
10. Top with fried onions and serve.

Serving Suggestions: Fresh salad will accompany this casserole nicely.

Variation Tip: Any kind of fresh mushrooms can be used.

Nutritional Information per Serving:

Calories: 125|**Fat:** 8.6g|**Sat Fat:** 2g|**Carbohydrates:** 11g|**Fiber:** 4.2g|**Sugar:** 2.4g|**Protein:** 3g

Potato Gratin

Preparation Time: 15 minutes | **Cooking Time:** 20 minutes
Servings: 4

Ingredients:

- 2 large potatoes, sliced thinly
- 5½ tablespoons cream
- 2 eggs
- 1 tablespoon plain flour
- ½ cup cheddar cheese, grated

Preparation:

1. Press "Power Button" of Ninja Foodi Digital Air Fry Oven and turn the dial to select "Air Fry" mode.
2. Press "Time Button" and again turn the dial to set the cooking time to 10 minutes.
3. Now push "Temp Button" and rotate the dial to set the temperature at 355 degrees F.
4. Press "Start/Pause" button to start.
5. When the unit beeps to show that it is preheated, open the lid.
6. Arrange the potato slices in the air fry basket and insert in the oven.
7. Meanwhile, in a bowl, add cream, eggs and flour and mix until a thick sauce forms.
8. When cooking time is complete, open the lid and remove the potato slices from the basket.
9. Divide the potato slices in 4 ramekins evenly and top with the egg mixture evenly, followed by the cheese.
10. Press "Power Button" of Ninja Foodi Digital Air Fry Oven and turn the dial to select "Air Fry" mode.
11. Press "Time Button" and again turn the dial to set the cooking time to 10 minutes.
12. Now push "Temp Button" and rotate the dial to set the temperature at 390 degrees F.
13. Arrange the ramekins in the air fry basket and insert in the oven.
14. Press "Start/Pause" button to start.
15. When cooking time is complete, open the lid and remove the ramekins from the oven.
16. Serve warm.

Serving Suggestions: Serve this gratin with fresh lettuce.

Variation Tip: Make sure to cut the potato slices thinly.

Nutritional Information per Serving:

Calories: 233 | **Fat:** 8g | **Sat Fat:** 4.3g | **Carbohydrates:** 31.3g | **Fiber:** 4.5g | **Sugar:** 2.7g | **Protein:** 9.7g

Veggie Ratatouille

Preparation Time: 15 minutes
Cooking Time: 15 minutes
Servings: 4

Ingredients:

- 1 green bell pepper, seeded and chopped
- 1 yellow bell pepper, seeded and chopped
- 1 eggplant, chopped
- 1 zucchini, chopped
- 3 tomatoes, chopped
- 2 small onions, chopped
- 2 garlic cloves, minced
- 2 tablespoons Herbs de Provence
- 1 tablespoon olive oil
- 1 tablespoon balsamic vinegar
- Salt and freshly ground black pepper, to taste

Preparation:

1. In a large bowl, add the vegetables, garlic, Herbs de Provence, oil, vinegar, salt, and black pepper and toss to coat well.
2. Transfer vegetable mixture into a greased baking pan.
3. Press "Power Button" of Ninja Foodi Digital Air Fry Oven and turn the dial to select "Air Fry" mode.
4. Press "Time Button" and again turn the dial to set the cooking time to 15 minutes.
5. Now push "Temp Button" and rotate the dial to set the temperature at 355 degrees F.
6. Press "Start/Pause" button to start.
7. When the unit beeps to show that it is preheated, open the lid.
8. Arrange the pan over the wire rack and insert in the oven.
9. When cooking time is complete, open the lid and place the pan aside for about 5 minutes before serving.

Serving Suggestions: Serve ratatouille over a cooked grain, such as rice, quinoa, or pasta.

Variation Tip: Make sure to use fresh veggies.

Nutritional Information per Serving:

Calories: 119|**Fat:** 4.2g|**Sat Fat:** 0.6g|**Carbohydrates:** 20.3g|**Fiber:** 7.3g|**Sugar:** 11.2g|**Protein:** 3.6g

Vegetarian Loaf

Preparation Time: 20 minutes
Cooking Time: 1½ hours
Servings: 6

Ingredients:

- 1 (14½-ounce) can vegetable broth
- ¾ cup brown lentils, rinsed
- 1 tablespoon olive oil
- 1¾ cups carrots, peeled and shredded
- 1 cup fresh mushrooms, chopped
- 1 cup onion, chopped
- 1 tablespoon fresh parsley, minced
- 1 tablespoon fresh basil, minced
- ½ cup cooked brown rice
- 1 cup mozzarella cheese, shredded
- 1 large egg
- 1 large egg white
- Salt and freshly ground black pepper, to taste
- 2 tablespoons tomato paste
- 2 tablespoons water

Preparation:

1. In a pan, place the broth over medium-high heat and bring to a boil.
2. Stir in the lentils and again bring to a boil.
3. Reduce the heat to low and simmer, covered for about 30 minutes.
4. Remove from the heat and set aside to cool slightly.
5. Meanwhile, in a large skillet, heat the oil over medium heat and sauté the carrots, mushrooms and onion for about 10 minutes.
6. Stir in herbs and remove from the heat.
7. Transfer the veggie mixture into a large bowl and set aside to cool slightly.
8. After cooling, add the lentils, rice, cheese, egg, egg white and seasonings and lentils and mix until well combined.
9. In a small bowl, stir together the tomato paste and water.
10. Place the mixture into a greased parchment paper-lined loaf pan and top with water mixture.
11. Press "Power Button" of Ninja Foodi Digital Air Fry Oven and turn the dial to select "Air Bake" mode.
12. Press "Time Button" and again turn the dial to set the cooking time to 50 minutes.
13. Now push "Temp Button" and rotate the dial to set the temperature at 350 degrees F.
14. Press "Start/Pause" button to start.

15. When the unit beeps to show that it is preheated, open the lid.
16. Arrange the loaf pan over the wire rack and insert in the oven.
17. When cooking time is complete, open the lid and place the loaf pan onto a wire rack for about 10 minutes before slicing.
18. Carefully invert the loaf onto the wire rack.
19. Cut into desired sized slices and serve.

Serving Suggestions: Serve this loaf with fresh baby greens.

Variation Tip: You can also use green lentils instead of brown lentils.

Nutritional Information per Serving:

Calories: 229|**Fat:** 5.1g|**Sat Fat:** 1.3g|**Carbohydrates:** 33.4g|**Fiber:** 9.4g|**Sugar:** 4g|**Protein:** 12.8g

Veggie Kabobs

Preparation Time: 20 minutes
Cooking Time: 10 minutes
Servings: 6

Ingredients:

- ¼ cup carrots, peeled and chopped
- ¼ cup French beans
- ½ cup green peas
- 1 teaspoon ginger
- 3 garlic cloves, peeled
- 3 green chilies
- ¼ cup fresh mint leaves
- ½ cup cottage cheese
- 2 medium boiled potatoes, mashed
- ½ teaspoon five-spice powder
- Salt, to taste
- 2 tablespoons corn flour
- Olive oil cooking spray

Preparation:

1. In a food processor, add the carrot, beans, peas, ginger, garlic, mint, cheese and pulse until smooth.
2. Transfer the mixture into a bowl.
3. Add the mashed potatoes, five-spice powder, salt and corn flour and with your hands mix until well combined.
4. Shape the mixture into equal-sized small balls.
5. Press each ball around a skewer in a sausage shape.
6. Spray the skewers with cooking spray.
7. Press "Power Button" of Ninja Foodi Digital Air Fry Oven and turn the dial to select "Air Fry" mode.
8. Press "Time Button" and again turn the dial to set the cooking time to 10 minutes.
9. Now push "Temp Button" and rotate the dial to set the temperature at 390 degrees F.
10. Press "Start/Pause" button to start.
11. When the unit beeps to show that it is preheated, open the lid and grease the air fry basket.
12. Arrange the skewers into the prepared air fry basket and insert in the oven.
13. When cooking time is complete, open the lid and transfer the skewers onto a platter.
14. Serve warm.

Serving Suggestions: Enjoy these kabobs wt yogurt dip.

Variation Tip: You can add spices of your choice in these veggie kabobs

Nutritional Information per Serving:

Calories: 120, **Fat:** 0.8g|**Sat Fat:** 0.3g| **Carbohydrates:** 21.9g|**Fiber:** 4.9g|**Sugar:** 1.8g| **Protein:** 6.3g

Stuffed Pumpkin

Preparation Time: 20 minutes
Cooking Time: 30 minutes
Servings: 5

Ingredients:

- 1 sweet potato, peeled and chopped
- 1 parsnip, peeled and chopped
- 1 carrot, peeled and chopped
- ½ cup fresh peas, shelled
- 1 onion, chopped
- 2 garlic cloves, minced
- 1 egg, beaten
- 2 teaspoons mixed dried herbs
- Salt and freshly ground black pepper, to taste
- ½ of butternut pumpkin, seeded

Preparation:

1. In a large bowl, mix together the vegetables, garlic, egg, herbs, salt, and black pepper.
2. Stuff the pumpkin half with vegetable mixture.
3. Press "Power Button" of Ninja Foodi Digital Air Fry Oven and turn the dial to select "Air Fry" mode.
4. Press "Time Button" and again turn the dial to set the cooking time to 30 minutes.
5. Now push "Temp Button" and rotate the dial to set the temperature at 355 degrees F.
6. Press "Start/Pause" button to start.
7. When the unit beeps to show that it is preheated, open the lid.
8. Arrange the pumpkin half into the air fry basket and insert in the oven.
9. When cooking time is complete, open the lid and transfer the pumpkin onto a serving platter.
10. Set aside to cool slightly before serving.

Serving Suggestions: Serve with the topping of fresh pomegranate seeds.

Variation Tip: Change the stuffing to suit your tastes.

Nutritional Information per Serving:

Calories: 223|**Fat:** 1.3g|**Sat Fat:** 0.3g|**Carbohydrates:** 53g|**Fiber:** 9.9g|**Sugar:** 12g|**Protein:** 6g

Basil Tomatoes

Preparation Time: 10 minutes
Cooking Time: 10 minutes
Servings: 2

Ingredients:

- 3 tomatoes, halved
- Olive oil cooking spray
- Salt and freshly ground black pepper, to taste
- 1 tablespoon fresh basil, chopped

Preparation:

1. Drizzle the cut sides of the tomato halves with cooking spray evenly.
2. Then, sprinkle with salt, black pepper and basil.
3. Press "Power Button" of Ninja Foodi Digital Air Fry Oven and turn the dial to select "Air Fry" mode.
4. Press "Time Button" and again turn the dial to set the cooking time to 10 minutes.
5. Now push "Temp Button" and rotate the dial to set the temperature at 320 degrees F.
6. Press "Start/Pause" button to start.
7. When the unit beeps to show that it is preheated, open the lid.
8. Arrange the tomatoes into the air fry basket and insert in the oven.
9. When cooking time is complete, open the lid and transfer the tomatoes onto serving plates.
10. Serve warm.

Serving Suggestions: You can use these tomatoes in pasta and pasta salads with a drizzle of balsamic vinegar.

Variation Tip: Fresh thyme can also be used instead of basil.

Nutritional Information per Serving:

Calories: 34|**Fat:** 0.4g|**Sat Fat:** 0.1g|**Carbohydrates:** 7.2g|**Fiber:** 2.2g|**Sugar:** 4.9g|**Protein:** 1.7g

Parmesan Asparagus

Preparation Time: 10 minutes
Cooking Time: 10 minutes
Servings: 3

Ingredients:

- 1 pound fresh asparagus, trimmed
- 1 tablespoon Parmesan cheese, grated
- 1 tablespoon butter, melted
- 1 teaspoon garlic powder
- Salt and freshly ground black pepper, to taste

Preparation:

1. In a bowl, mix together the asparagus, cheese, butter, garlic powder, salt, and black pepper.
2. Press "Power Button" of Ninja Foodi Digital Air Fry Oven and turn the dial to select "Air Fry" mode.
3. Press "Time Button" and again turn the dial to set the cooking time to 10 minutes.
4. Now push "Temp Button" and rotate the dial to set the temperature at 400 degrees F.
5. Press "Start/Pause" button to start.
6. When the unit beeps to show that it is preheated, open the lid and grease the air fry basket.
7. Arrange the veggie mixture into the prepared air fry basket and insert in the oven.
8. When cooking time is complete, open the lid and transfer the asparagus onto serving plates.
9. Serve hot.

Serving Suggestions: Serve with the garnishing of pine nuts.

Variation Tip: you can use fresh garlic instead of garlic powder.

Nutritional Information per Serving:

Calories: 73|**Fat:** 4.4g|**Sat Fat:** 2.7g|**Carbohydrates:** 6.6g|**Fiber:** 3.3g|**Sugar:** 3.1g|**Protein:** 4.2g

Spicy Butternut Squash

Preparation Time: 10 minutes
Cooking Time: 20 minutes
Servings: 4

Ingredients:

- 1 medium butternut squash, peeled, seeded and cut into chunk
- 2 teaspoons cumin seeds
- 1/8 teaspoon garlic powder
- 1/8 teaspoon chili flakes, crushed
- Salt and freshly ground black pepper, to taste
- 1 tablespoon olive oil
- 2 tablespoons pine nuts
- 2 tablespoons fresh cilantro, chopped

Preparation:

1. In a bowl, mix together the squash, spices, and oil.
2. Press "Power Button" of Ninja Foodi Digital Air Fry Oven and turn the dial to select "Air Fry" mode.
3. Press "Time Button" and again turn the dial to set the cooking time to 20 minutes.
4. Now push "Temp Button" and rotate the dial to set the temperature at 375 degrees F.
5. Press "Start/Pause" button to start.
6. When the unit beeps to show that it is preheated, open the lid and grease the air fry basket.
7. Arrange the squash chunks into the prepared air fry basket and insert in the oven.
8. When cooking time is complete, open the lid and transfer the squash chunks onto serving plates.
9. Serve hot with the garnishing of pine nuts and cilantro.

Serving Suggestions: Serve with a sprinkle of sweet dried cranberries.

Variation Tip: you can microwave the butternut squash for 2-3 mins to make it softer and easier to remove the skin.

Nutritional Information per Serving:

Calories: 191|**Fat:** 7g|**Sat Fat:** 0.8g|**Carbohydrates:** 34.3g|**Fiber:** 6g|**Sugar:** 6.4g|**Protein:** 3.7g

Garlicky Brussels Sprout

Preparation Time: 12 minutes
Cooking Time: 15 minutes
Servings: 4

Ingredients:

- 1 pound Brussels sprouts, cut in half
- 2 tablespoons oil
- 2 garlic cloves, minced
- ¼ teaspoon red pepper flakes, crushed
- Salt and freshly ground black pepper, to taste

Preparation:

1. In a bowl, add all the ingredients and toss to coat well.
2. Press "Power Button" of Ninja Foodi Digital Air Fry Oven and turn the dial to select "Air Fry" mode.
3. Press "Time Button" and again turn the dial to set the cooking time to 12 minutes.
4. Now push "Temp Button" and rotate the dial to set the temperature at 390 degrees F.
5. Press "Start/Pause" button to start.
6. When the unit beeps to show that it is preheated, open the lid.
7. Arrange the Brussels sprouts into the air fry basket and insert in the oven.
8. When cooking time is complete, open the lid and transfer the Brussels sprouts onto serving plates.
9. Serve hot.

Serving Suggestions: Sprinkle with flaky sea salt before serving.

Variation Tip: Look for small to medium sprouts for better taste.

Nutritional Information per Serving:

Calories: 113|**Fat:** 9g|**Sat Fat:** 1.3g|**Carbohydrates:** 8.3g|**Fiber:** 2.6g|**Sugar:** 4.2g|**Protein:** 2.8g

Glazed Mushrooms

Preparation Time: 10 minutes
Cooking Time: 15 minutes
Servings: 4

Ingredients:

- ¼ cup soy sauce
- ¼ cup honey
- ¼ cup balsamic vinegar
- 2 garlic cloves, chopped finely
- ½ teaspoon red pepper flakes, crushed
- 18 ounces fresh Cremini mushrooms, halved

Preparation:

1. In a bowl, place the soy sauce, honey, vinegar, garlic and red pepper flakes and mix well. Set aside.
2. Place the mushroom into the greased baking pan in a single layer.
3. Press "Power Button" of Ninja Foodi Digital Air Fry Oven and turn the dial to select "Air Bake" mode.
4. Press "Time Button" and again turn the dial to set the cooking time to 15 minutes.
5. Now push "Temp Button" and rotate the dial to set the temperature at 350 degrees F.
6. Press "Start/Pause" button to start.
7. When the unit beeps to show that it is preheated, open the lid.
8. Insert the baking pan in oven.
9. After 8 minutes of cooking, place the honey mixture in baking pan and toss to coat well.
10. When cooking time is complete, open the lid and transfer the mushrooms onto serving plates.
11. Serve hot.

Serving Suggestions: Topping of fresh chives or marjoram gives a delish touch to mushrooms.

Variation Tip: Maple syrup will be an excellent substitute for honey.

Nutritional Information per Serving:

Calories: 113|**Fat:** 0.2g|**Sat Fat:** 0g|**Carbohydrates:** 24.7g|**Fiber:** 1g|**Sugar:** 20g|**Protein:** 4.4g

Chapter 7: Dessert Recipes

Banana Split

Preparation Time: 15 minutes
Cooking Time: 14 minutes
Servings: 8

Ingredients:

- 3 tablespoons coconut oil
- 1 cup panko breadcrumbs
- ½ cup corn flour
- 2 eggs
- 4 bananas, peeled and halved lengthwise
- 3 tablespoons sugar
- ¼ teaspoon ground cinnamon
- 2 tablespoons walnuts, chopped

Preparation:

1. In a medium skillet, melt the coconut oil over medium heat and cook breadcrumbs for about 3-4 minutes or until golden browned and crumbled, stirring continuously.
2. Transfer the breadcrumbs into a shallow bowl and set aside to cool.
3. In a second bowl, place the corn flour.
4. In a third bowl, whisk the eggs.
5. Coat the banana slices with flour and then, dip into eggs and finally, coat with the breadcrumbs evenly.
6. In a small bowl, mix together the sugar and cinnamon.
7. Press "Power Button" of Ninja Foodi Digital Air Fry Oven and turn the dial to select "Air Fry" mode.
8. Press "Time Button" and again turn the dial to set the cooking time to 10 minutes.
9. Now push "Temp Button" and rotate the dial to set the temperature at 280 degrees F.
10. Press "Start/Pause" button to start.
11. When the unit beeps to show that it is preheated, open the lid.
12. Arrange the banana slices into the air fry basket and sprinkle with cinnamon sugar.
13. Insert the basket in the oven.
14. When cooking time is complete, open the lid and transfer the banana slices onto plates to cool slightly
15. Sprinkle with chopped walnuts and serve.

Serving Suggestions: Serve with a scoop of strawberry ice cream.

Variation Tip: Pecans will be an excellent substitute for walnuts.

Nutritional Information per Serving:

Calories: 216|**Fat:** 8.8g|**Sat Fat:** 5.3g|**Carbohydrates:** 26g|**Fiber:** 2.3g|**Sugar:** 11.9g|**Protein:** 3.4g

Nutty Pears

Preparation Time: 10 minutes
Cooking Time: 30 minutes
Servings: 2

Ingredients:

- 1 ripe Anjou pear, halved and cored
- 1/8 teaspoon ground cinnamon
- 6 semisweet chocolate chips
- 2 tablespoons pecans, chopped
- 1 teaspoon pure maple syrup

Preparation:

1. Arrange the pear halves onto the greased sheet pan cut sides up and sprinkle with cinnamon.
2. Top each half with chocolate chips and pecans and drizzle with maple syrup.
3. Arrange a rack in the bottom position of Ninja Foodi Digital Air Fry Oven.
4. Press "Power Button" of Ninja Foodi Digital Air Fry Oven and turn the dial to select "Air Fry" mode.
5. Press "Time Button" and again turn the dial to set the cooking time to 30 minutes.
6. Now push "Temp Button" and rotate the dial to set the temperature at 350 degrees F.
7. Press "Start/Pause" button to start.
8. When the unit beeps to show that it is preheated, open the lid and insert the sheet pan in the oven.
9. When cooking time is complete, open the lid and transfer the pears onto a platter.
10. Serve warm.

Serving Suggestions: Sweet whipped cream will go great with these pears.

Variation Tip: Choose firm pears with the stem intact.

Nutritional Information per Serving:

Calories: 111|**Fat:** 6g|**Sat Fat:** 0.9g|**Carbohydrates:** 15g|**Fiber:** 3.1g|**Sugar:** 9.9g|**Protein:** 1.2g

Glazed Figs

Preparation Time: 10 minutes
Cooking Time: 10 minutes
Servings: 4

Ingredients:

- 4 fresh figs
- 4 teaspoons honey
- 2/3 cup Mascarpone cheese, softened
- Pinch of ground cinnamon

Preparation:

1. Cut each fig into the quarter, leaving just a little at the base to hold the fruit together.
2. Arrange the figs onto a parchment paper-lined sheet pan and drizzle with honey.
3. Place about 2 teaspoons of Mascarpone cheese in the center of each fig and sprinkle with cinnamon.
4. Press "Power Button" of Ninja Foodi Digital Air Fry Oven and turn the dial to select the "Air Broil" mode.
5. Press "Time Button" and again turn the dial to set the cooking time to 10 minutes.
6. Press "Start/Pause" button to start.
7. When the unit beeps to show that it is preheated, open the lid and insert the sheet pan in oven.
8. When cooking time is complete, open the lid and transfer the figs onto a platter.
9. Serve warm.

Serving Suggestions: Topping of chopped nuts will add a nice nutty texture.

Variation Tip: Select figs that are clean and dry, with smooth, unbroken skin.

Nutritional Information per Serving:

Calories: 141|**Fat:** 5.5g|**Sat Fat:** 3.5g|**Carbohydrates:** 19.2g|**Fiber:** 1.9g|**Sugar:** 15g|**Protein:** 5.3g

Citrus Mousse

Preparation Time: 15 minutes
Cooking Time: 12 minutes
Servings: 2

Ingredients:

For Mousse:

- 4 ounces cream cheese, softened
- ½ cup heavy cream
- 2 tablespoons fresh lime juice
- 2 tablespoons maple syrup
- Pinch of salt

For Topping:

- 2 tablespoons heavy whipping cream

Preparation:

1. For mousse: in a bowl, add all the ingredients and mix until well combined.
2. Transfer the mixture into 2 ramekins.
3. Press "Power Button" of Ninja Foodi Digital Air Fry Oven and turn the dial to select "Air Bake" mode.
4. Press "Time Button" and again turn the dial to set the cooking time to 12 minutes.
5. Now push "Temp Button" and rotate the dial to set the temperature at 350 degrees F.
6. Press "Start/Pause" button to start.
7. When the unit beeps to show that it is preheated, open the lid.
8. Arrange the ramekins over the wire rack and insert in the oven. When cooking time is complete, open the lid and place the ramekins aside to cool.
9. Refrigerate the ramekins for at least 3 hours before serving.
10. Top with heavy whipping cream and serve.

Serving Suggestions: serve with a garnishing of banana slices.

Variation Tip: Make sure to use freshly squeezed juice.

Nutritional Information per Serving:

Calories: 354|**Fat:** 30.9g|**Sat Fat:** 19.4g|**Carbohydrates:** 15.9g|**Fiber:** 0g|**Sugar:** 12g|**Protein:** 4.9g

Chocolate Pudding

Preparation Time: 20 minutes
Cooking Time: 12 minutes
Servings: 4

Ingredients:

- ½ cup butter
- 2/3 cup dark chocolate, chopped
- ¼ cup caster sugar
- 2 medium eggs
- 2 teaspoons fresh orange rind, finely grated
- ¼ cup fresh orange juice
- 2 tablespoons self-rising flour

Preparation:

1. In a microwave-safe bowl, add the butter and chocolate and microwave on high heat for about 2 minutes or until melted completely, stirring after every 30 seconds.
2. Remove from the microwave and stir the mixture until smooth.
3. Add the sugar and eggs and whisk until frothy.
4. Add the orange rind and juice, followed by flour and mix until well combined.
5. Divide mixture into 4 greased ramekins about ¾ full.
6. Press "Power Button" of Ninja Foodi Digital Air Fry Oven and turn the dial to select "Air Fry" mode.
7. Press "Time Button" and again turn the dial to set the cooking time to 12 minutes.
8. Now push "Temp Button" and rotate the dial to set the temperature at 355 degrees F.
9. Press "Start/Pause" button to start.
10. When the unit beeps to show that it is preheated, open the lid.
11. Arrange the ramekins into the air fry basket and insert in the oven.
12. When cooking time is complete, open the lid and place the ramekins set aside to cool completely before serving.

Serving Suggestions: Serve with the garnishing of fresh strawberries and mint leaves.

Variation Tip: This pudding can be served chilled too.

Nutritional Information per Serving:

Calories: 454|**Fat:** 33.6g|**Sat Fat:** 21.1g|**Carbohydrates:** 34.2g|**Fiber:** 1.2g|**Sugar:** 28.4g|**Protein:** 5.7g

Red Velvet Cupcakes

Preparation Time: 20 minutes
Cooking Time: 12 minutes
Servings: 12

Ingredients:

For Cupcakes:

- 2 cups refined flour
- ¾ cup icing sugar
- 2 teaspoons beet powder
- 1 teaspoon cocoa powder
- ¾ cup peanut butter
- 3 eggs

For Frosting:

- 1 cup butter
- 1 (8-ounce) package cream cheese, softened
- 2 teaspoons vanilla extract
- ¼ teaspoon salt
- 4½ cups powdered sugar

For Garnishing:

- ½ cup fresh raspberries

Preparation:

1. For cupcakes: in a bowl, add all the ingredients and with an electric whisker, whisk until well combined.
2. Place the mixture into silicone cups.
3. Press "Power Button" of Ninja Foodi Digital Air Fry Oven and turn the dial to select "Air Fry" mode.
4. Press "Time Button" and again turn the dial to set the cooking time to 12 minutes.
5. Now push "Temp Button" and rotate the dial to set the temperature at 340 degrees F.
6. Press "Start/Pause" button to start.
7. When the unit beeps to show that it is preheated, open the lid.
8. Arrange the silicone cups into the air fry basket and insert in the oven.
9. When cooking time is complete, open the lid and place the silicone cups onto a wire rack to cool for about 10 minutes.
10. Carefully invert the cupcakes onto the wire rack to completely cool before frosting.
11. For frosting: in a large bowl, mix well butter, cream cheese, vanilla extract, and salt.
12. Add the powdered sugar, one cup at a time, whisking well after each addition.
13. Spread frosting over each cupcake.
14. Garnish with raspberries and serve.

Serving Suggestions: Garnishing of sprinkles will add a festive touch in cupcakes.

Variation Tip: Measure the ingredients with care.

Nutritional Information per Serving:

Calories: 599|**Fat:** 31.5g, |**Sat Fat:** 16g|**Carbohydrates:** 73.2g|**Fiber:** 2g|**Sugar:** 53.4g|**Protein:** 9.3g

Chocolate Mug Cake

Preparation Time: 10 minutes
Cooking Time: 17 minutes
Servings: 2

Ingredients:

- ¼ cup flour
- 2 tablespoons sugar
- ¼ teaspoon baking powder
- 1/8 teaspoon baking soda
- 1/8 teaspoon salt
- 2 tablespoons milk
- 2 tablespoons applesauce
- ½ tablespoon vegetable oil
- ¼ teaspoon vanilla extract
- 2 tablespoons chocolate chips

Preparation:

1. In a bowl, mix together the flour, sugar, baking powder, baking soda and salt.
2. Add the milk, applesauce, oil and vanilla extract and mix until well combined.
3. Gently, fold in the chocolate chips.
4. Place the mixture into an over proof mug.
5. Press "Power Button" of Ninja Foodi Digital Air Fry Oven and turn the dial to select "Air Bake" mode.
6. Press "Time Button" and again turn the dial to set the cooking time to 17 minutes.
7. Now push "Temp Button" and rotate the dial to set the temperature at 375 degrees F.
8. Press "Start/Pause" button to start.
9. When the unit beeps to show that it is preheated, open the lid.
10. Arrange the mug over the wire rack and insert in the oven.
11. When cooking time is complete, open the lid and place the mug onto a wire rack to cool for about 10 minutes.
12. Serve warm.

Serving Suggestions: Sprinkle the cake with powdered sugar before serving.

Variation Tip: Use the best quality chocolate chips for cake.

Nutritional Information per Serving:

Calories: 204|**Fat:** 7g|**Sat Fat:** 3.1g|**Carbohydrates:** 33g|**Fiber:** 1g|**Sugar:** 19.8g|**Protein:** 2.9g

Plum Crisp

Preparation Time: 15 minutes
Cooking Time: 40 minutes
Servings: 2

Ingredients:

- 1½ cups plums, pitted and sliced
- ¼ cup sugar, divided
- 1½ teaspoons cornstarch
- 3 tablespoons flour
- ¼ teaspoon ground cinnamon
- Pinch of salt
- 1½ tablespoons cold butter, chopped
- 3 tablespoons rolled oats

Preparation:

1. In a bowl, place plum slices, 1 teaspoon of sugar and cornstarch and toss to coat well.
2. Divide the plum mixture into lightly greased 2 (8-ounce) ramekins.
3. In a bowl, mix together the flour, remaining sugar, cinnamon and salt.
4. With a pastry blender, cut in bitterer until a crumbly mixture forms.
5. Add the oats and gently stir to combine.
6. Place the oat mixture over plum slices into each ramekin.
7. Press "Power Button" of Ninja Foodi Digital Air Fry Oven and turn the dial to select "Air Bake" mode.
8. Press "Time Button" and again turn the dial to set the cooking time to 40 minutes.
9. Now push "Temp Button" and rotate the dial to set the temperature at 350 degrees F.
10. Press "Start/Pause" button to start.
11. When the unit beeps to show that it is preheated, open the lid.
12. Arrange the ramekins over the wire rack and insert in the oven.
13. When cooking time is complete, open the lid and place the ramekins onto a wire rack to cool for about 10 minutes.
14. Serve warm.

Serving Suggestions: Vanilla ice cream will go great with crisp.

Variation Tip: Select plums with a sweet aroma and free of bruises and faded spots.

Nutritional Information per Serving:

Calories: 273|**Fat:** 9.4g|**Sat Fat:** 5.6g|**Carbohydrates:** 47.2g|**Fiber:** 1.9g|**Sugar:** 30.4g|**Protein:** 2.7g

Vanilla Cheesecake

Preparation Time: 15 minutes
Cooking Time: 14 minutes
Servings: 6

Ingredients:

- 1 cup honey graham cracker crumbs
- 2 tablespoons unsalted butter, softened
- 1 pound cream cheese, softened
- ½ cup sugar
- 2 large eggs

Preparation:

1. Line a round baking pan with parchment paper.
2. For crust: in a bowl, add the graham cracker crumbs and butter.
3. Place the crust into the baking dish and press to smooth.
4. Press "Power Button" of Ninja Foodi Air Fry Oven and turn the dial to select the "Air Fry" mode.
5. Press "Time Button" and again turn the dial to set the cooking time to 4 minutes.
6. Now push "Temp Button" and rotate the dial to set the temperature at 350 degrees F.
7. Press "Start/Pause" button to start.
8. When the unit beeps to show that it is preheated, open the lid.
9. Arrange the baking pan of crust into the air fry basket and insert in the oven.
10. When cooking time is complete, open the lid and place the crust aside to cool for about 10 minutes.
11. Meanwhile, in a bowl, add the cream cheese and sugar and whisk until smooth.
12. Now, place the eggs, one at a time and whisk until the mixture becomes creamy.
13. Add the vanilla extract and mix well.
14. Place the cream cheese mixture over the crust evenly.
15. Press "Power Button" of Ninja Foodi Air Fry Oven and turn the dial to select the "Air Fry" mode.
16. Press "Time Button" and again turn the dial to set the cooking time to 10 minutes.
17. Now push "Temp Button" and rotate the dial to set the temperature at 350 degrees F.
18. Press "Start/Pause" button to start.
19. When the unit beeps to show that it is preheated, open the lid.
20. Arrange the baking pan into the air fry basket and insert in the oven.
21. When cooking time is complete, open the lid and place the pan onto a wire rack to cool completely.
22. Refrigerate overnight before serving.

Serving Suggestions: Serve with the topping of fresh berries.

Variation Tip: Your cream cheese should always be at room temperature.

Nutritional Information per Serving:

Calories: 470|**Fat:** 33.9g|**Sat Fat:** 20.6g|**Carbohydrates:** 349g|**Fiber:** 0.5g|**Sugar:** 22g|**Protein:** 9.4g

3 Weeks Meal Plan:

Week 1

Day 1:

Breakfast: Ham Brie Sandwich

Lunch: Italian Turkey Breast

Snack: Sweet Potato Fries

Dinner: Lobster Tail

Dessert: Molten Lava Cake

Day 2:

Breakfast: Breakfast Hash

Lunch: Thanksgiving Turkey Meal

Snack: Corn on the Cob

Dinner: Garlic Parmesan Shrimp

Dessert: Crispy Oreos

Day 3:

Breakfast: Breakfast Frittata

Lunch: Turkey Meatloaf

Snack: Calzones

Dinner: Cajun Shrimp

Dessert: Cinnamon Rolls

Day 4:

Breakfast: Chile-Cheese Frittata

Lunch: General Tso's Chicken

Snack: Pita Pizzas

Dinner: Mangalorean Fish Fry

Dessert: Sweet Apples

Day 5:

Breakfast: Hasselback Potatoes

Snack: Spanakopita Bites

Lunch: Chicken Enchiladas

Dinner: Lemon Shrimp and Vegetables

Dessert: Bread Pudding

Day 6:

Breakfast: Morning Bagels

Lunch: Korean Chicken Wings

Snack: Pork Dumplings

Dinner: Shrimp and Crab Casserole

Dessert: Carrot Cake

Day 7:

Breakfast: Egg Avocado Boats

Lunch: Cheesy Chicken Nachos

Snack: Curry Chickpeas

Dinner: Crusted Tilapia

Dessert: Glazed Donut

Week 2

Day 1:

Breakfast: Ham Brie Sandwich

Lunch: Bacon Wrapped Shrimp

Snack: Sweet Potato Fries

Dinner: Italian Pasta Bake

Dessert: Molten Lava Cake

Day 2:

Breakfast: Breakfast Hash

Lunch: Sheet Pan Tofu Dinner

Snack: Turkey Croquettes

Dinner: Sausage Casserole

Dessert: Crispy Oreos

Day 3:

Breakfast: Breakfast Frittata

Lunch: Eggplant Parmesan

Snack: Pork Meatballs

Dinner: Christmas Casserole

Dessert: Cinnamon Rolls

Day 4:

Breakfast: Chile-Cheese Frittata

Lunch: Herbed Potato, Asparagus, and Chickpea

Snack: Crab Rangoon

Dinner: Bacon Meatloaf

Dessert: Sweet Apples

Day 5:

Breakfast: Hasselback Potatoes

Lunch: Porcini Mac and Cheese

Snack: Spanakopita Bites

Dinner: Steak Bites Mushrooms

Dessert: Bread Pudding

Day 6:

Breakfast: Morning Bagels

Lunch: Spicy Cauliflower Stir-Fry

Snack: Pork Dumplings

Dinner: Glazed Steaks

Dessert: Carrot Cake

Day 7:

Breakfast: Egg Avocado Boats

Lunch: Sheet Pan Fajitas

Snack: Kale Salad with Roasted Veggies

Dinner: Herbed Lamb Chops

Dessert: Glazed Donut

Week 3

Day 1:

Breakfast: Breakfast Bombs

Lunch: Artichoke Spinach Casserole

Snack: Kale and Potato Nuggets

Dinner: Lamb Chops with Garlic Sauce

Dessert: French Toast Sticks with Berries

Day 2:

Breakfast: Egg Avocado Boats

Lunch: Chicken, Sweet Potatoes and Broccoli

Snack: Cinnamon Apple Chips

Dinner: Lamb Sirloin Steak

Dessert: Fudgy Brownies

Day 3:

Breakfast: Chile-Cheese Frittata

Lunch: Chicken Sheet Pan Meal

Snack: Corn Dog Bites

Dinner: Tofu Butternut Squash Dinner

Dessert: Strawberry Roll Cake

Day 4:

Breakfast: Chile-Cheese Frittata

Lunch: General Tso's Chicken

Snack: Pita Pizzas

Dinner: Masala Chops

Dessert: Sweet Apples

Day 5:

Breakfast: Hasselback Potatoes

Lunch: Chicken Enchiladas

Snack: Spanakopita Bites

Dinner: Sheet Pan Pork with Apples

Dessert: Bread Pudding

Day 6:

Breakfast: Morning Bagels

Lunch: Korean Chicken Wings

Snack: Pork Dumplings

Dinner: Cauliflower pork casserole

Dessert: Carrot Cake

Day 7:

Breakfast: Egg Avocado Boats

Lunch: Cheesy Chicken Nachos

Snack: Curry Chickpeas

Dinner: Holiday Ham

Dessert: Glazed Donut

Conclusion

The Ninja Foodi Digital Air Fry Oven gives you a whole new experience of convenient cooking by bringing a variety of cooking styles into a single appliance. Where the Ninja foodi guarantees effective cooking with minimal supervision, this cookbook ensures that you get the most out of your Ninja Foodi Air Fry oven by developing its better understanding and by trying all sorts of recipes, including breakfasts, poultry, meat, snacks, seafood, and desserts, which are all shared in different chapters of this cookbook. With its single read, all the Ninja Foodi Air Fry oven beginners can readily learn basic techniques to bake and cook like a pro.

Remember, when you are done cooking with this digital oven, make sure to clean it thoroughly before putting it away. Thankfully the cleaning is quite when it comes to the Ninja Air Fryer ovens, especially when it comes to SP101 because due to its flip design, you can easily make it stand and open the lower power to remove the crumb tray and clean the oven inside out. After every session, the screen will show the "Red" hot sign on the screen until it is cooled. The moment it is cooled down, the screen shows a "Flip" sign, and the Hot sign disappears. Unplug the device carefully to cut off the power supply. Now remove all the removable items from inside the oven that may include the sheet pan, the wire rack, the Air Fryer basket, and crumb tray. Wash these removable items in the dishwasher or using the soapy water. Let them dry to use again. Hold the handle under the lid and flip the oven by pushing its front upward. Pull the base of the oven, and it will come out like the lid. Wipe off the base with the help of a wet cloth. Allow its base to dry out completely, then close it.

So, if you really want to avail all the smart cooking feature offered by this amazing cooking appliance, then it's about time that you adorn your kitchen counter with this smartly designed multipurpose oven, and then start cooking some magic at home using our special Ninja digital Air Fry oven recipe collection.

www.ingramcontent.com/pod-product-compliance
Lightning Source LLC
Chambersburg PA
CBHW080627170426
43209CB00007B/1535

スペシャルサンクス

ジミー バス、ダーシー ライト、チャーリー バナコス、
そして我が妻マドカ、彼女の変わらぬ愛情とサポートへ。
この本を息子ジェイムス オメガ ムーニーに捧げる。

Copyright © WATERFALL PUBLISHING HOUSE 2011

This title is published by Waterfall Publishing House
Astoria, New York USA 11102

All Rights Reserved
No part of this publication may be produced, stored in a retrieval
system or transmitted in any form or means, photocopying, mechanical or
electronic without prior written permission of Waterfall Publishing House.

Print Edition ISBN 978-1-937187-15-6
Ebook   ISBN 978-1-937187-16-3

Library of Congress Control Number: 2011928126

Japanese Print Edition ISBN 978-1-937187-18-7
Japanese Ebook Print Edition ISBN 978-1-937187-20-0

Musical Score : Jazz
Musical Score : Studies & exercises, etudes

Japanese translation by Shinya Yonezawa
Editing by Madoka Mooney
翻訳者　米澤　信哉
編集　　マドカ　ムーニー

Layout and music engraving by Steven Mooney
Cover Design by Steven Mooney

©Waterfall Publishing House 2011

コンストラクティング　ウォーキング　ジャズ　ベースラインズ　ブックIII

スタンダード ラインズ

ウォーキング　ジャズ　ベースラインズを構築する為の
コンプリートガイド

エレクトリックベース対応

ベースタブ譜エディション

著者 STEVEN MOONEY
スティーブン　ムーニー

カバーデザイン　スティーブン　ムーニー

©Waterfall Publishing House 2011

序文

　エレクトリックベーシストに向けた、コンストラクティングウォーキングジャズベースラインシリーズの第3巻であるスタンダードラインズは、ジャズスタンダードにおいて、ウォーキングベースラインを組み立てるのに使われる、様々な手法を幅広く紹介した内容になっています。

　第3巻では、演奏例として、110コーラスのベースラインが、24のスタンダードジャズコード進行で紹介されています。

　パートⅠでは、モードとコードスケールの関係、そして全ての調性において、ダイアトニックトライアドとセブンスコードを組み立てるのに必要な、基礎的な知識を説明しています。演奏例は、ベーシストが、しっかりとしたリズムとハーモニーの基礎を養えるように、"2フィール"と"4フィール"のウォーキングベースのスタイルで紹介されています。
　ボイスリーディングと、モードのサブスティチューション、特定のジャズコード進行に対するモードの適用等を含む、より高度なベースラインの構築の例も紹介されています。
　パートⅡでは、シンメトリックスケールおよびマイナーⅡⅤⅠ進行に関連した、メロディックマイナースケールから派生するモードについて述べられています。ここで紹介されているものは、シンメトリックスケールとコードスケールの関係、そして一般的なジャズコード進行に対する、シンメトリックスケールの使い方になります。またよくあるジャズコード進行上で、マイナーⅡⅤⅠに対して一般的に使われるスケールの紹介と共に、メジャーⅡⅤⅠとの違いについて述べています。
　パートⅢでは、よくあるジャズコード進行上での、ビバップスケールの使い方を紹介しています。
　パートⅣでは、それまでに述べられた様々な手法やコンセプトを用い、スタンダードジャズコード進行において、プロフェッショナルレベルのベースラインの例を紹介しています。

　本書で網羅されている全ての手法は、ベーシストがそれらのテクニックを12キーに適用できるように、一歩一歩段階的に紹介されています。

©Waterfall Publishing House 2011

©Waterfall Publishing House 2011

目次

Part 1

コードスケールの関係 .... p. 9
スタンダードコード進行に対する、モードおよび
コードスケールの関係の適用方法 .... p. 10
メジャースケールからトライアドを取り出す方法 .... p. 14
ジャズコード進行#1 "Periodic"
ベースラインの構築、トライアドと"2"フィール .... p. 15
トライアドによる"4"フィールウォーキングベースライン .... p. 16
トライアドと上方からのクロマティックアプローチノート .... p. 18
トライアドと下方からのクロマティックアプローチノート .... p. 22
トライアドとウォークアップ .... p. 25
トライアドとウォークダウン .... p. 26
ジャズコード進行#2 "Greatest Glove"
ベースライン構築の音階的アプローチ（上昇形） .... p. 28
音階的ベースラインにセブンスコードを適用する
ダイアトニックセブンスの作り方 .... p. 30
音階的ベースラインにセブンスコードを適用する（下降形） .... p. 31
上昇する音階的ラインと上からのクロマティックアプローチ .... p. 32
下降する音階的ラインと下からのクロマティックアプローチ .... p. 34
セブンスコードのボイスリーディングとⅡⅤⅠ進行 .... p. 36
ジャズコード進行#3 "Winters Coming"
ベースラインにボイスリーディングのテクニックを適用する .... p. 37
ドミナントセブンスコードのボイスリーディング .... p. 40

ウォーキングジャズベースラインに対するモードの適用方法
イオニアンモード .... p. 46
ジャズコード進行#4 "Mr. K" .... p. 47

目次

メジャーⅡⅤⅠ進行とドリアン、ミクソリディアンモード ……………… p. 49
ⅡⅤⅠ進行 …………………………………………………………………… p. 50
ジャズコード進行におけるⅡⅤⅠ進行の適用 …………………………… p. 51
Ⅲ Ⅵ Ⅱ Ⅴ進行とフリジアンモード ………………………………………… p. 53
Ⅲ Ⅵ Ⅱ Ⅴ Ⅰ進行 …………………………………………………………… p. 54
ジャズコード進行におけるⅢ Ⅵ Ⅱ Ⅴ Ⅰ進行の適用 …………………… p. 55
Ⅰ Ⅵ Ⅱ Ⅴ進行とエオリアンモード ……………………………………… p. 57
ジャズコード進行におけるⅠ Ⅵ Ⅱ Ⅴ進行の適用 ……………………… p. 59
リディアンモード ………………………………………………………… p. 61
ジャズコード進行#5 "It Depends"
ベースライン構築にリディアンモードを適用する ……………………… p. 62
ロクリアンモード ………………………………………………………… p. 69
ジャズコード進行#6 "The Weaving Stream"
ベースライン構築にロクリアンモードを適用する ……………………… p. 70

パートⅡ
シンメトリック、メロディックマイナースケール ……………………… p. 76
ホールトーンスケール
ジャズコード進行#7 "Wheres The Subway"
ジャズベースラインにおけるホールトーンスケールの適用 …………… p. 77
ディミニッシュドスケール ………………………………………………… p. 85
ジャズコード進行#8 "Finding Candy"
ジャズベースラインにおけるディミニッシュドスケールの適用 ……… p. 86
ハーフホールディミニッシュドスケール ………………………………… p. 92
ジャズコード進行#9 "Vegetable Stew"
ジャズベースラインにおける
ハーフホールディミニッシュドスケールの適用 ………………………… p. 93

©Waterfall Publishing House 2011

目次

ディミニッシュドホールトーンスケールとマイナー II V進行 .... p. 99
ジャズコード進行#10　"Moonlight View"
ジャズベースラインにおける
ディミニッシュドホールトーンスケールの適用................ p. 100
ロクリアン#2とマイナーII V進行................ p. 104
ジャズベースラインにおけるロクリアン#2の適用................ p. 105
マイナーII V進行................ p. 110

パート III
ビバップスケール
上昇するメジャービバップスケール................ p. 113
下降するメジャービバップスケール................ p. 114
ジャズコード進行#11　"More Stew?"
ジャズベースラインにおけるメジャービバップスケールの適用................ p. 115
上昇するドリアンマイナービバップスケール................ p. 121
下降するドリアンマイナービバップスケール................ p. 122
ジャズコード進行#12　"Heard It"
ジャズベースラインにおける
ドリアンマイナービバップスケールの適用................ p. 123
上昇するミクソリディアンビバップスケール................ p. 130
下降するミクソリディアンビバップスケール................ p. 131
ジャズコード進行#13　"Who's Glove"
ベースラインにおけるミクソリディアンビバップスケールの適用........ p. 132

パートIV　スタンダードジャズコード進行における、
ベースライン例................ p. 139
ジャズコード進行#14　"Ocean St"................ p. 140
ジャズコード進行#15　"Slipped into the Stream"................ p. 146
ジャズコード進行#16　"Only You"................ p. 152

©Waterfall Publishing House 2011

目次

ジャズコード進行 #17　" The One in Gloves " .... p. 158

ジャズコード進行 #18　" Garden Hoses " .... p. 164

ジャズコード進行 #19　" Who Are You ? " .... p. 171

ジャズコード進行 #20　" Idiosyncrasy " .... p. 179

ジャズコード進行 #21　" The Third " .... p. 185

ジャズコード進行 #22　" New Gloves " .... p. 190

ジャズコード進行 #23　" Bring Your Strings " .... p. 196

ジャズコード進行 #24　" No Ones Here " .... p. 203

終わりに臨んで .... p. 211

©Waterfall Publishing House 2011

パート1　コードスケールの関係

Standard Line Vol.I

スタンダードコード進行に対する、モードおよびコードスケールの関係の適用方法

モードとコードスケールの実践的な知識を持っていると、演奏されるハーモニーや、コードの構造が、より明確に認識できるようになるでしょう。

例えて言うなら、ベーシストが、あるコード進行を初めて見た時、それをただ単にAmin7 D7の1小節があり、次にGmin7　C7となってFmaj7になる、と見るか、この一連のコード進行を、FのキーにおけるⅢⅥⅡⅤの進行と見るか、という違いのことです。
曲を分析したり、暗譜をしようとする際に、曲の調性を把握できることや、モード、言い換えればコードスケールがどのように働くかを知っておくと、コードを一つ一つ単体で見るより、かなり楽に考えることが出来るでしょう。バンド上で曲を移調する時の助けにもなります。

次の例では、Fmajのキーにおける2オクターブの、モード（コードスケール）及びアルペジオが示されています。

F イオニアンモード

F maj7 アルペジオ

G ドリアンモード

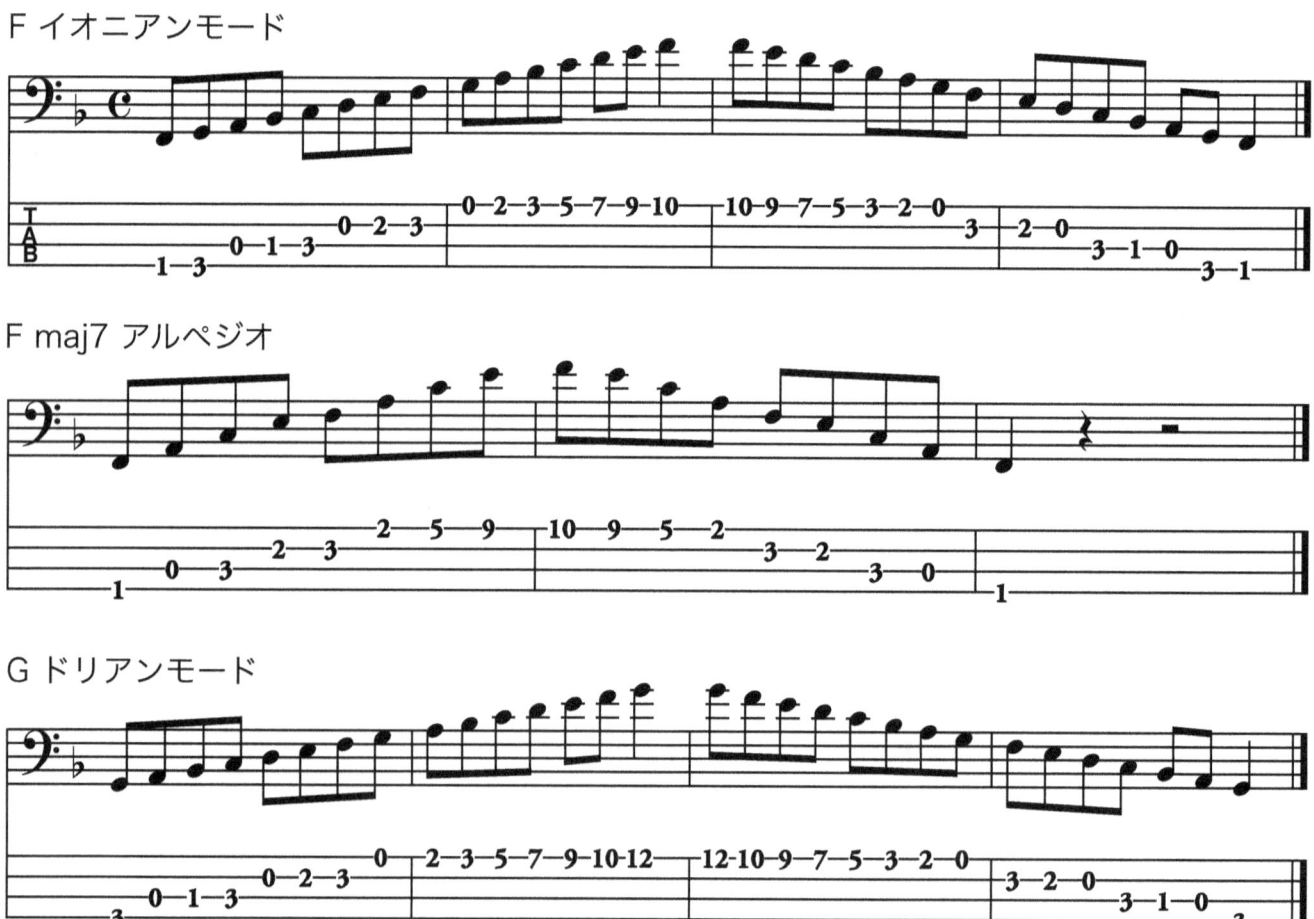

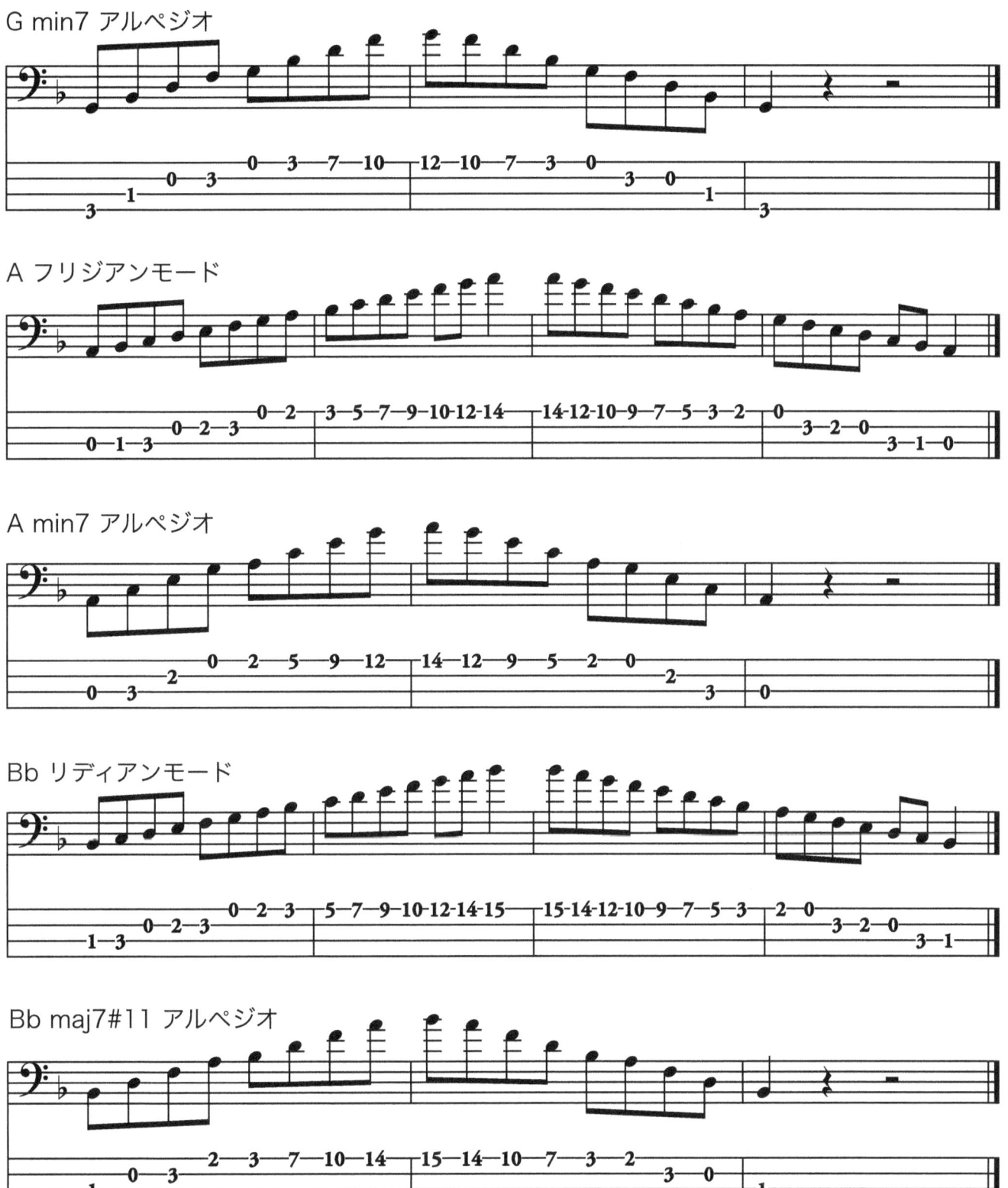

Standard Line Vol.I

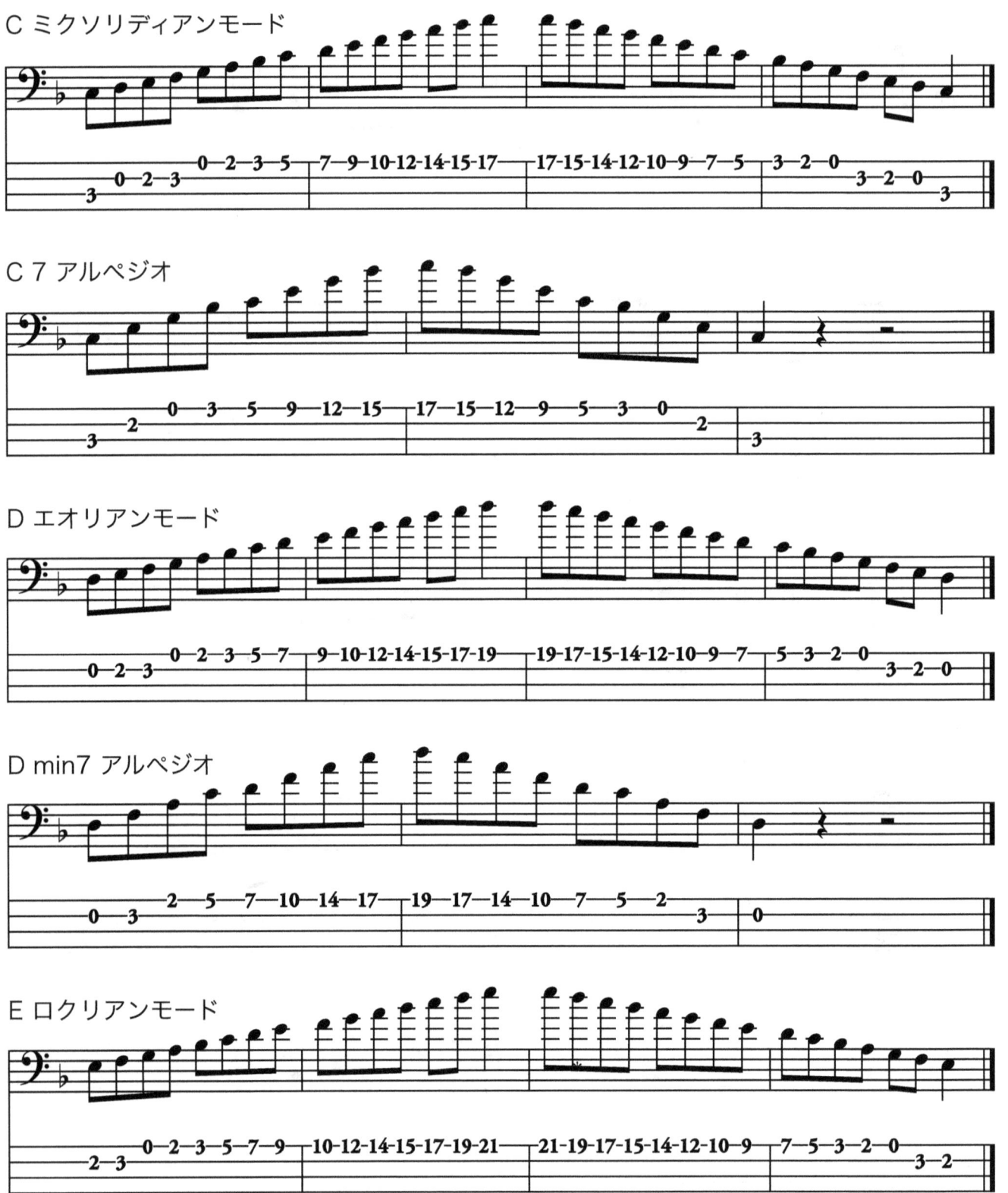

E ハーフディミニッシュアルペジオ

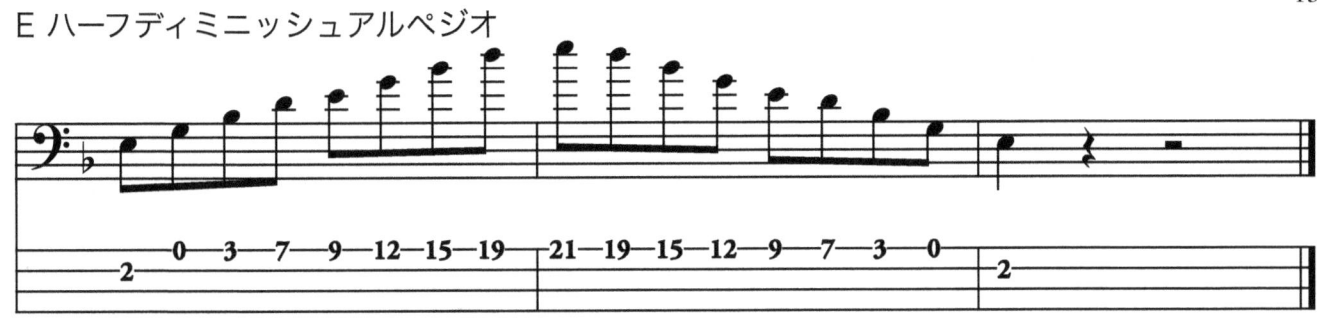

Standard Line Vol.I

メジャースケールからトライアドを取り出す方法

下記の例は、どのようにして、メジャースケールからダイアトニックトライアドを作っていくかを示していると同時に、モードを理解し、それらを調性に適用していく上で、最初のステップでもあります。

ベーシストにとって、ウォーキングベースラインを作っていく上で、トライアドを使うことには多くの利点があり、色々な領域を一度に学ぶことができると言えるでしょう。

まず第一に、トライアドは、コード進行を輪郭づくります。低音域において、トライアドが弾かれることによって、ソロイストは、しっかりしたハーモニーの基礎の上に演奏することが出来ますし、ギタリストやピアニストは、より上の音程で、テンション（緊張音）のサウンドを鳴らすことが出来るので、全体として、バンドのサウンドに厚みを与えることが出来ます。

第二に、楽器の低音域でトライアドを弾くことは、フレットを扱う手の物理的な強化、スタミナをつけることにもつながります。

第三に、ダブルベース奏者、或はフレットレスのエレクトリックベース奏者にとっては、トライアドを低音域で弾くことは、音程を整えるという意味において、最高のエクササイズだと言えるでしょう。ブルースや、スタンダードのコード進行で、オープンポジションから、ハーフステップ以上動くことなく、どんなキーでもウォーキングできるということは、望むべくことです。（ダブルベーシストにとっては、最初のポジションとハーフステップのポジションのことを表します）

トライアドを作るには、スケール上のどの音からも、2音間隔で音を取るところから始めます。例えば、F, A, C / G, Bb, D / A, C, E 等。

例1　1オクターブのFメジャースケール

例2　Fメジャースケールより作られた、FのキーのダイアトニックトライアドI

＊このVコードは♭7th（短7度）を足すと、ドミナントコードになります。

©Waterfall Publishing House 2011

"PERIODIC"　　　　　　　ジャズコード進行#1

例1は、楽器の低音域を使い、全般にわたり、トライアド（コードの第1、3、5音）から作られた基礎的な"2"フィールのベースラインを示しています。

Standard Line Vol.I

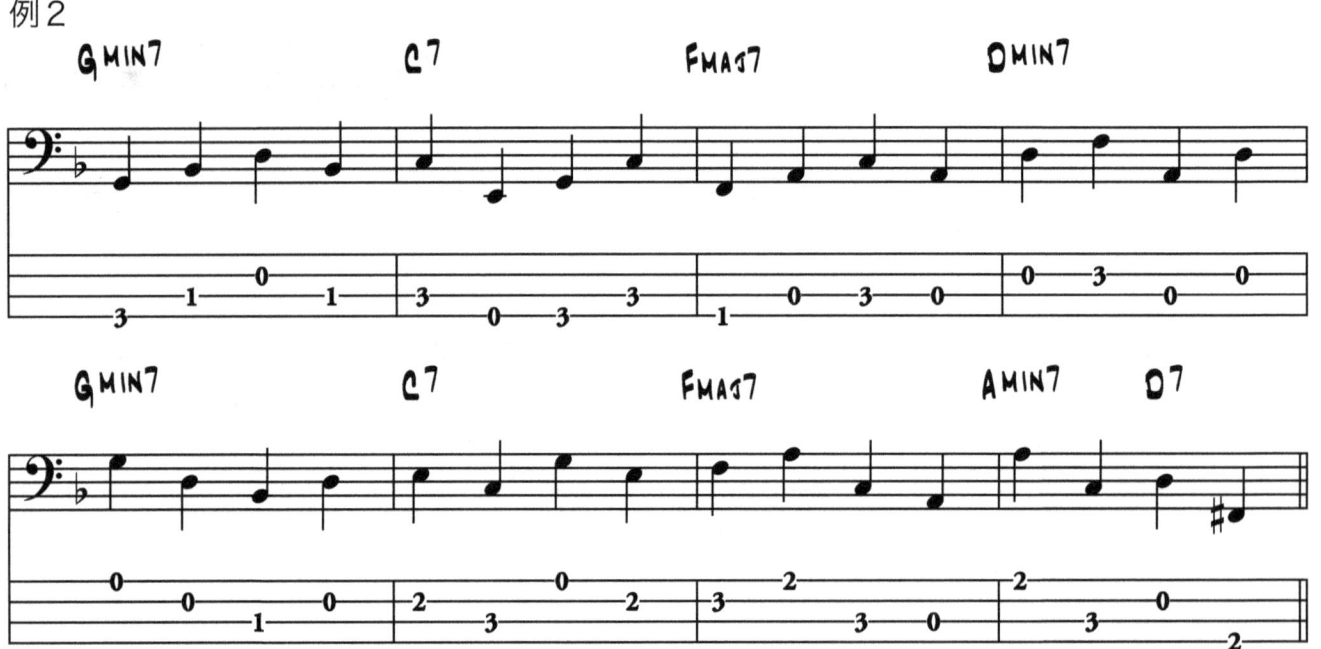

例 2 は 前頁のスタンダード（Periodic）のコード進行を、トライアドと、4 フィール（ウォーキングベースライン）を使って書かれたものです。

例 2

©Waterfall Publishing House 2011

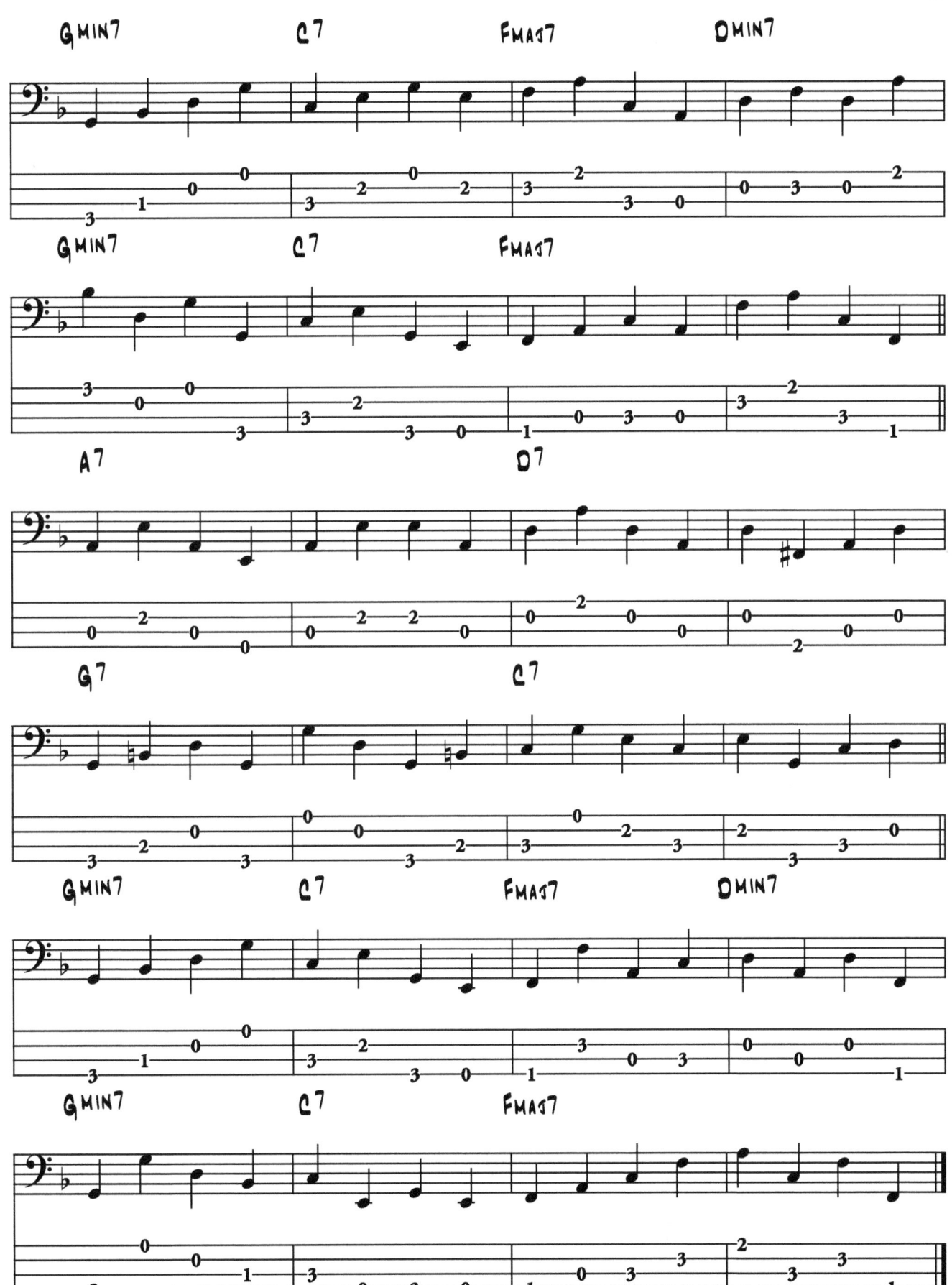

トライアドと上方からのクロマティック（半音階）アプローチノート

次の例は、上方からのクロマティックアプローチノートと呼ばれる、和声的な手法の使い方が示されています。

クロマティックアプローチノートは、ウォーキングベースラインに輪郭や、クロマティックアプローチノートが、コードトーンに解決することで、緊張と緩和の効果を与えるのに使われます。

コードトーンを、ダウンビート、1拍と3拍に維持するのにも役立つでしょう。

下の例は、トライアドと、上方からのクロマティックアプローチを用いた"2フィール"のベースベースラインを表しています。

Standard Line Vol.I

次は、トライアドと、上方からのクロマティックアプローチを使って作られた、ウォーキングベースライン（4フィール）の例を表しています。

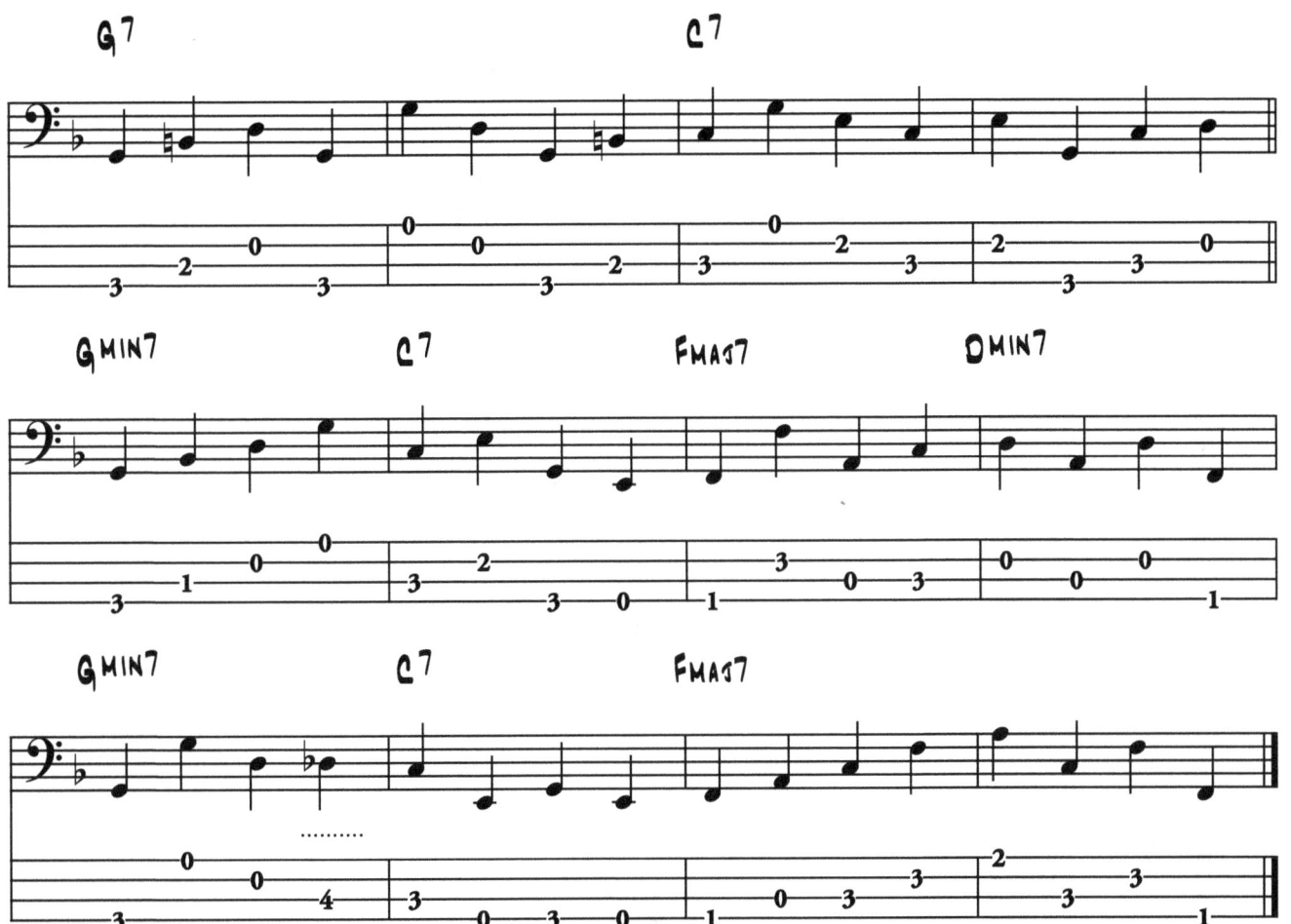

クロマティックアプローチノート＝..........

Standard Line Vol.I

トライアドと下方からのクロマティックアプローチノート

次は、下方からのクロマティックアプローチの例になります。
同じく、ベースラインに輪郭及び、緊張と緩和の効果を与えるのに使われ、コードトーンを、ダウンビート（1拍、3拍）に維持しておくことにも役立ちます。

下の例の1コーラス目は、トライアドと、下方からのクロマティックアプローチを用いた、"2フィール"のベースラインを表しています。2コーラス目は"4フィール"のウォーキングベースラインになります。

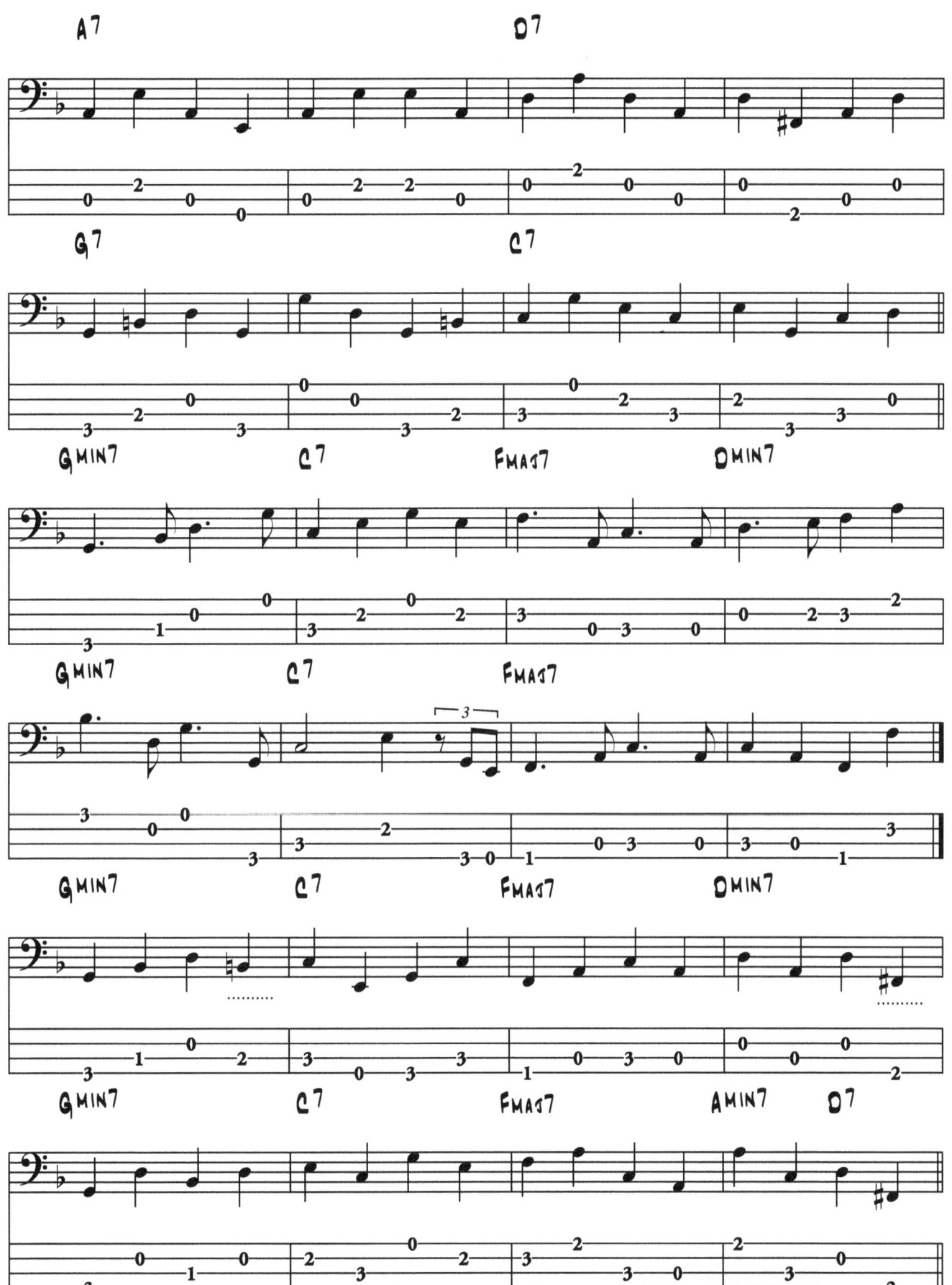

23

Standard Line Vol.I

クロマティックアプローチノート＝..........

トライアドとウォークアップ

次に述べるのは、これも一般的なウォーキングベースの手法で、ウォークアップと呼ばれます。2つのアプローチノートを使って、次のコードに下方からアプローチする手法です。

Aセクションの第1小節目が、このウォークアップです。6小節目にはC7コード上において、バリエーションが見られます。クロマティックノートがC音とD音の間で、2拍目で使われています。

Standard Line Vol.I

トライアドとウォークダウン

次も同じく、2つのアプローチノートを使って、今度は上方から次のコードにアプローチする手法、ウォークダウンです。

セカンドAセクションの2小節目と、最後のAセクションの2小節目に、ウォークダウンがあります。

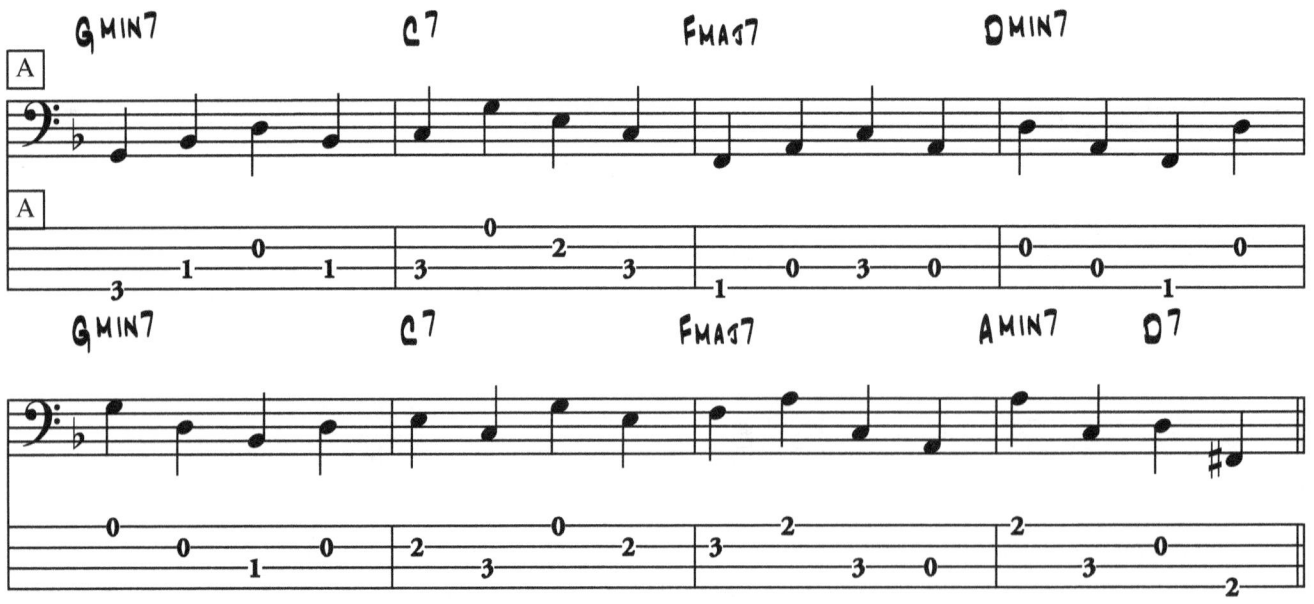

©Waterfall Publishing House 2011

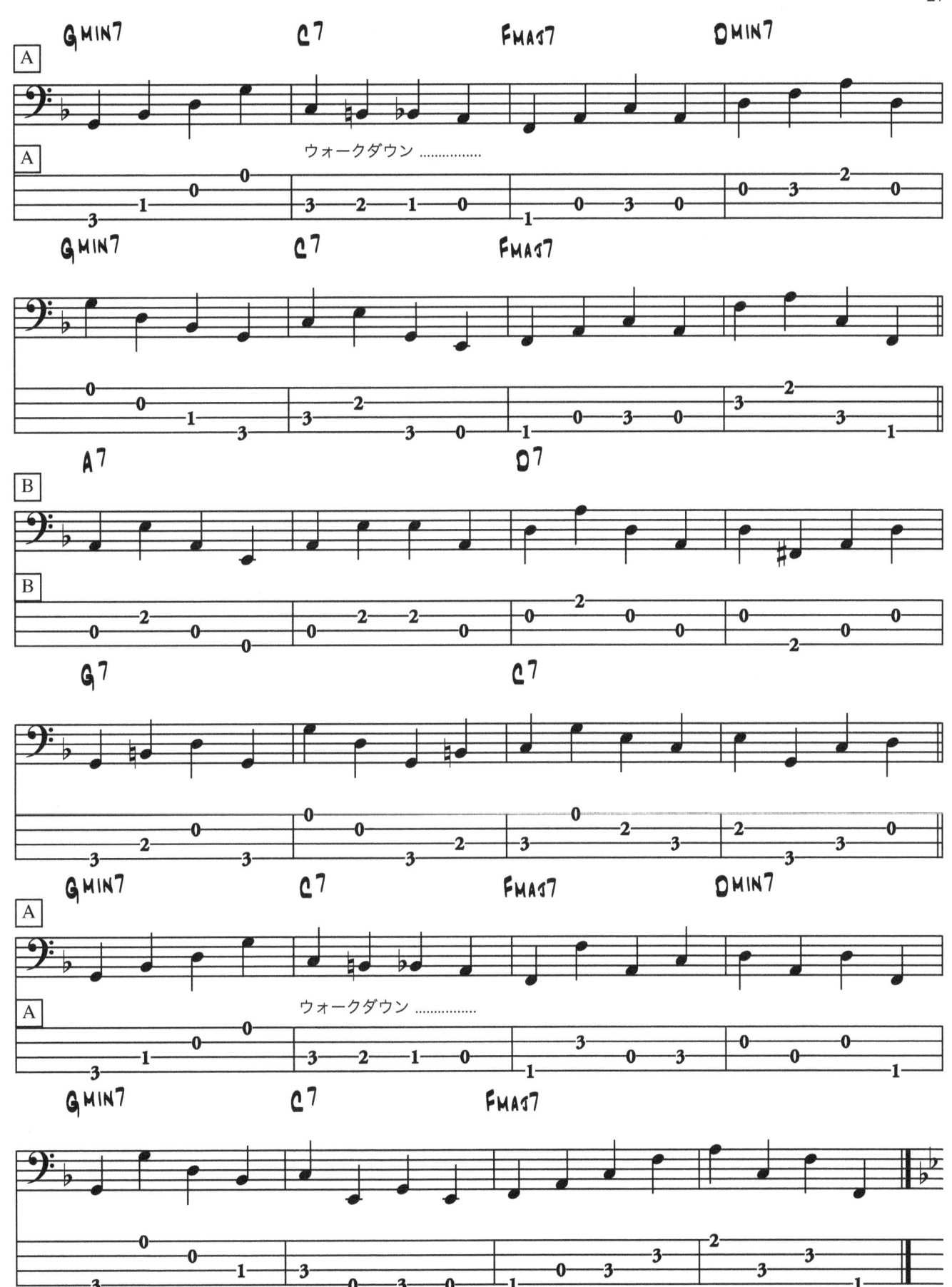

Standard Line Vol.I

" GREATEST GLOVE "

ジャズコード進行 #2

ベースライン構築の音階的アプローチ（上昇形）

スケール（音階）的なアプローチによるウォーキングベースラインは、より横軸のアプローチであり、そのベースラインは、よりスムーズな形になります。トライアドを使ってラインを作る代わりに、この例においては、スケールの音1、2、3、5音（1235の順列）を使ってラインを作っていきます。トライアドはバリエーションとして用います。
下の例は、それらを使ったAセクションに"2フィール"、Bセクションに"4フィール"のウォーキングベースラインです。

©Waterfall Publishing House 2011

1、2、3、5音を使った音階的アプローチ、もしくはそのバリエーション例=............

音階的ベースラインにセブンスコードを適用する

ダイアトニックセブンスの作り方

次の例は、メジャースケールから、どのようにしてセブンスコードを組み立てるかを、表しています。

例1　B♭メジャースケール

例2　B♭メジャースケールから組み立てられたダイアトニックトライアド

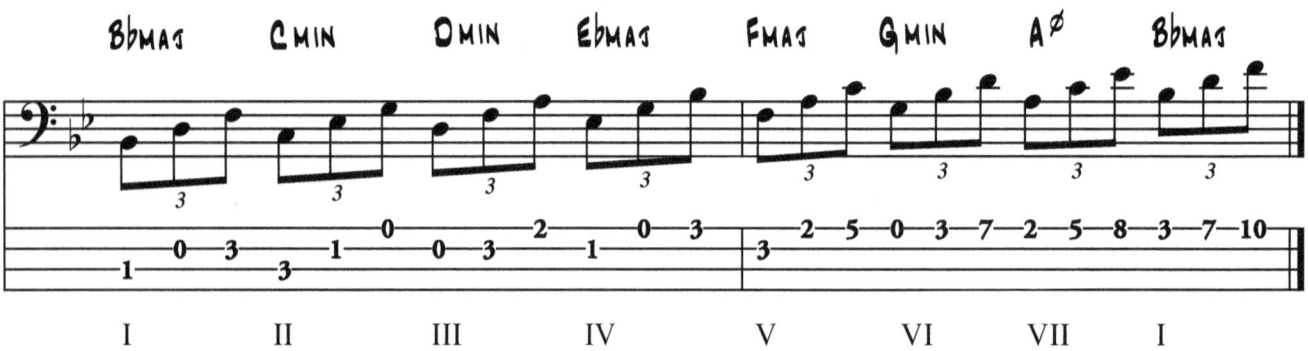

例3　B♭メジャースケールから組み立てられたダイアトニックセブンスコード

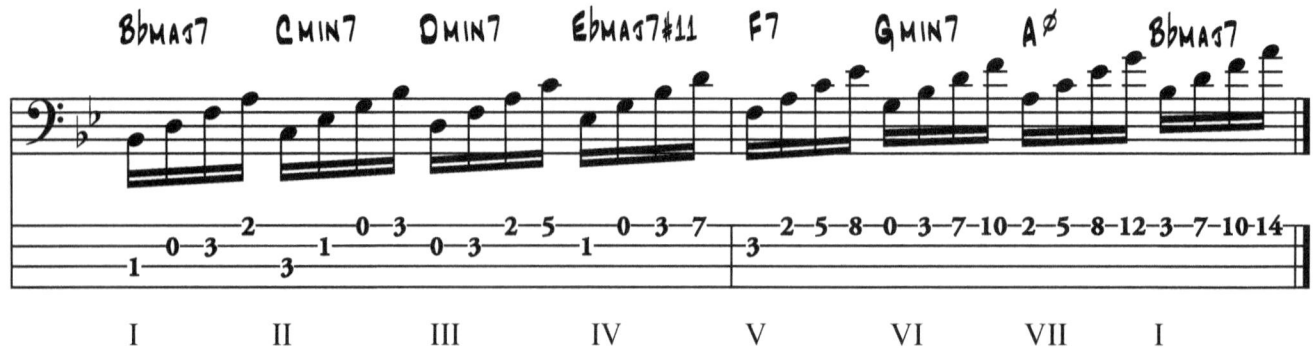

音階的ジャズベースラインにセブンスコードを適用する（下降形）

次の例は、ルート音から下降するスケールの音を使った（スケールの音1，7，6，5）音階的なアプローチの使い方を示しています。
この例では、他にトライアドと、上昇する音階的アプローチの手法も使われています。
ハーモニーの色々な音を使えることによって、この例では、ベースラインがより変化に富み、より旋律的になっていることが分かるでしょう。

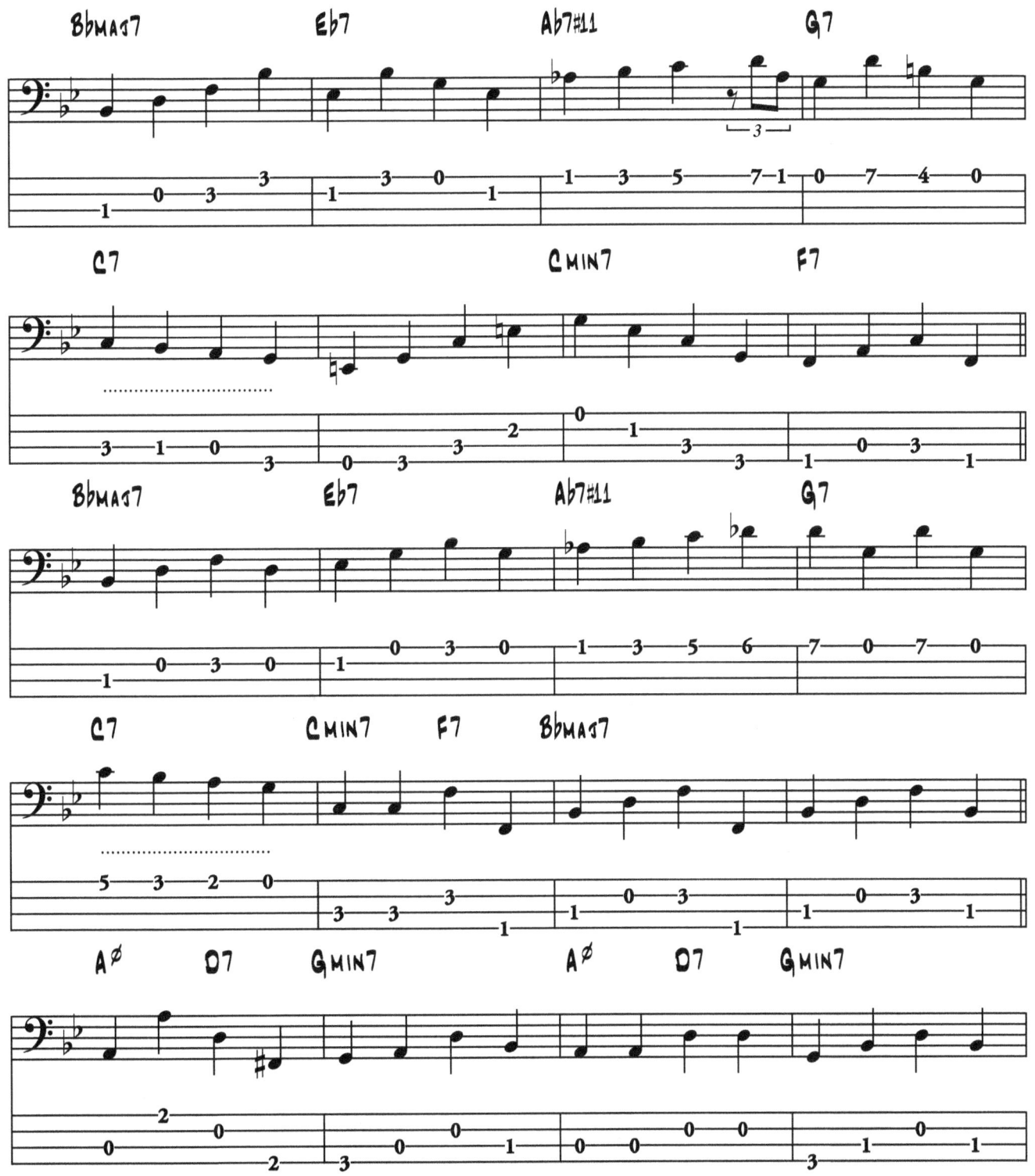

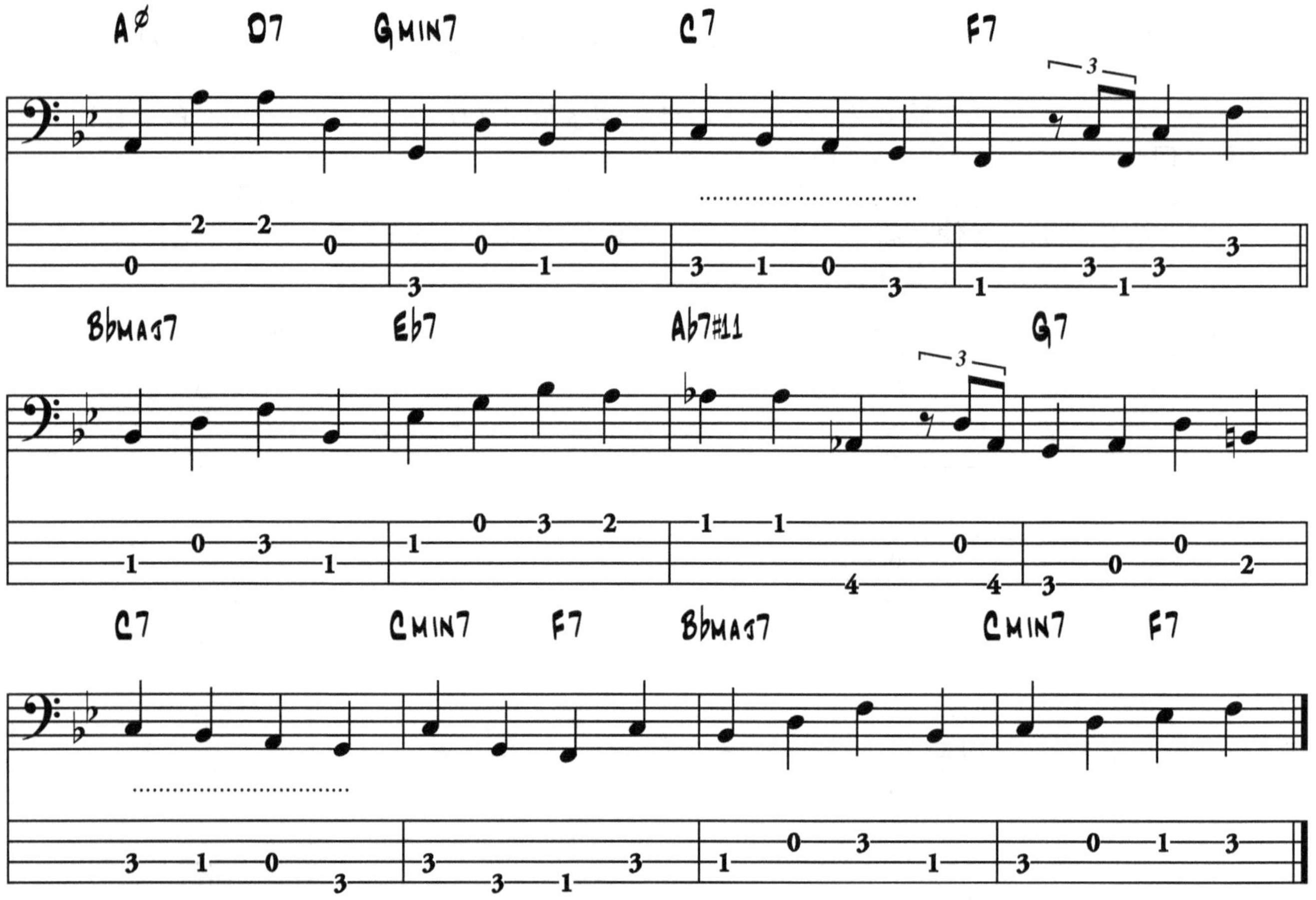

Standard Line Vol.I

1、7、6、5音を使った音階的アプローチ、もしくはそのバリエーション例=............

上昇する音階的ラインと上からのクロマティックアプローチ

続く例は、上方からのクロマティックアプローチを取り入れた、上昇する音階的なウォーキングベースラインを示しています。

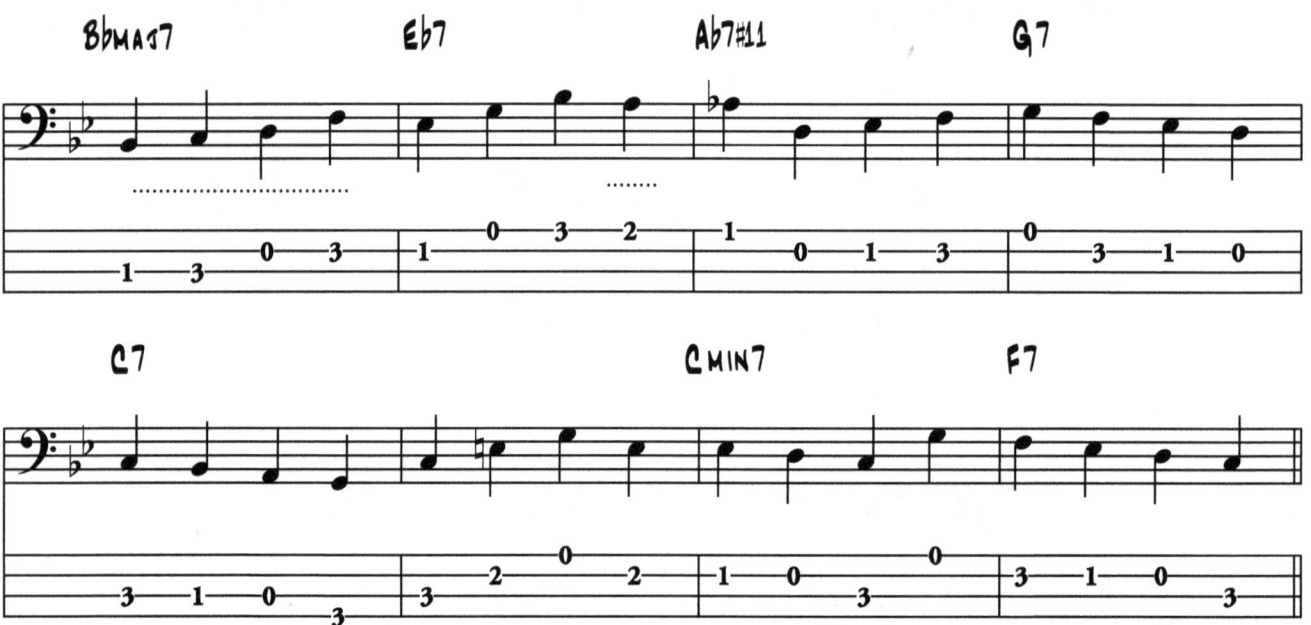

©Waterfall Publishing House 2011

Standard Line Vol.I

下降する音階的ラインと下からのクロマティックアプローチ

続く例は、下方からのクロマティックアプローチを取り入れた、下降する音階的なウォーキングベースラインを示しています。

*音階的ベースライン=................,クロマティックアプローチノート=.......

Standard Line Vol.1

セブンスコードのボイスリーディングとⅡⅤⅠ（ツーファイブワン）進行

続く例では、セブンスコードとボイスリーディングのテクニックを、ⅡⅤⅠ進行に組み入れていきます。このボイスリーディングのテクニックは、ここではIImin7コードとV7コードを繋ぐのに使われます。ボイスリーディングは全てのハーモニー楽器で使われる、大変効果的なテクニックです。
下の例のように、このテクニックを使うことによって、ベースラインは、ピアニストやギタリストがコードをボイシングすることとも、共有する部分が出てきます。

例1　B♭メジャーキーのⅡⅤⅠ進行です。

例2　Cmin7の♭7thであるB♭が、半音下がって、F7のmajor 3rdであるAに解決するというボイスリーディングの例。

例3　Cmin7の♭7thであるB♭が、全音上がって、F7の5thであるCに解決するというボイスリーディングの例。

ボイスリーディング例＝ ....

Standard Line Vol.I

ボイスリーディング例＝ ....

ドミナントセブンスコードのボイスリーディング

次の項では、ドミナントセブンスコードに対して適用された、ボイスリーディングのテクニックを示しています。

ボイスリーディングという用語は、コードトーンから、次のコードのコードトーンにステップワイズ（半音或は全音）で動くことを言います。

続く例では、B♭メジャーのキーでの、ボイスリーディングを示しています。

最初の例1は、B♭メジャーのⅡⅤⅠ進行のベースラインですが、F7のコードにおいて、ボイスリーディングは使われていません。

例 1

例 2　ボイスリーディングのテクニックが、2小節目のF7のコードで使われています。ここではF7の♭7thであるE♭が、B♭メジャーコードのmajor 3rdであるDに、半音下がって解決しています。

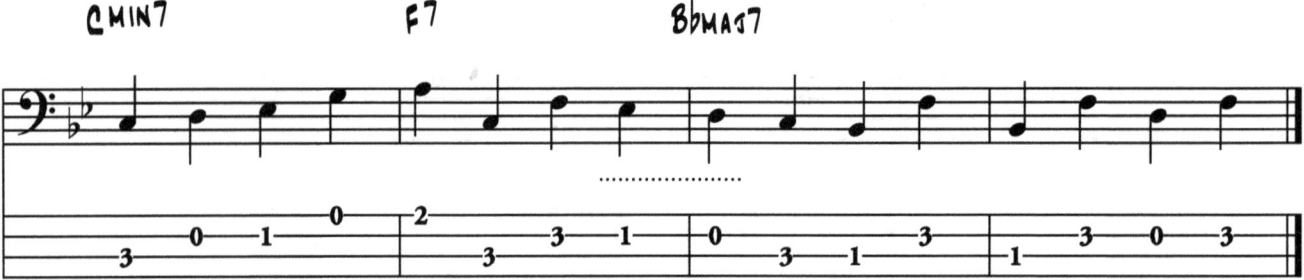

例 3　ボイスリーディングテクニックが、2小節目のF7において使われています。F7の♭7thであるE♭が全音上がって、B♭メジャーの5thであるFに解決しています。

ボイスリーディングのテクニックを用いることによって、ベースラインがより強力に前へ進む感覚を得て、さらにコード楽器がコードをボイシングする時の方法とも繋がりがでてきます。

続く"WINTERS COMING"におけるベースラインの例では、F7のコードでボイスリーディングを行っています。

" WINTERS COMING "　　　　　　ジャズコード進行#3

Standard Line Vol.I

Standard Line Vol.I

ボイスリーディング例＝ ....

Standard Line Vol.I

ウォーキングジャズベースラインに対するモードの適用方法

次のチャプターでは、ウォーキングベースラインに対するモードの使用方、及び機能的ジャズハーモニーの中で、コードスケールの見つけ方についての概説をしています。

最初のチャプターでは、モードと、その関連するスケール、アルペジオ、そしてどのようにして、メジャースケールからモードを作り出すかについて概説しました。

コードの構造や、どのようにコードが機能しているかが理解出来れば、（ⅠⅤⅠ、やⅡⅤⅠ、ⅠⅥⅡⅤなど）モードや、そのコードスケールを使っていけるようになります。

調性に対するモードを用いることによって、各小節に１コードずつ形づくるようなベースラインから離れて、調性全体で形作るようなより長いラインを作っていけるようになるでしょう。

結果としては、まるで異なったベースの旋律になりますが、どちらのアプローチも、コード進行の輪郭を形作りますし、コード進行を表現する有効な方法であることに違いはありません。ベーシストは、出来る限り多くの選択肢を身に付けておくべきです。そうすることで、様々なベースラインを用いることや、ソロイストに対して多彩なインスピレーションを提供する、という意味において、より自由になることが出来るでしょう。

イオニアンモード、或はⅠメジャーコード

次のスタンダードジャズ進行の "Mr. K" のコード進行は、Fメジャーのキーの、イオニアンモード、或はⅠメジャーコードの適用について表しています。

Fイオニアンモード

Fメジャーセブンアルペジオ

"MR. K" ジャズコード進行 #4

Standard Line Vol.I

イオニアンモードベースラインもしくはそのバリエーション例＝……………

メジャー II V I 進行とドリアン、ミクソリディアンモード

次の例は、ベースラインを形作る際の、ドリアン、ミクソリディアンモードの適用について表しています。

スタンダードコード進行の#4である、Fメジャーのキーの "Mr. K" は、II V I の進行を演奏する時の、ドリアン及びミクソリディアンモードの使用法を表しています。

下の例では、Fメジャーのキーに関係するドリアン及びミクソリディアンモードを表しています。

Gドリアンスケール

Gmin7　2オクターブアルペジオ

Cミクソリディアンスケール

C7　2オクターブアルペジオ

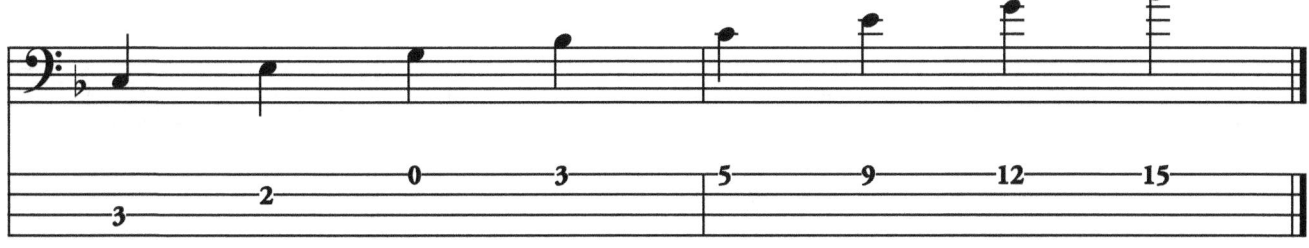

©Waterfall Publishing House 2011

ⅡⅤⅠ（ツーファイブワン）進行

ここからのチャプターでは、ⅡⅤⅠ進行と、ジャズハーモニーにおけるその機能についての概説をしています。このⅡⅤⅠの進行は、ジャズスタンダードのレパートリーの中でも、最も多く使われている進行のひとつであり、12キー全てで学ぶ必要があるものです。

ここでもう一度、ダイアトニックセブンスコードを参照してみれば（ここではFメジャーのキー）、ⅡⅤⅠという言葉の由来がよく分かります。

ⅡⅤ（ツーファイブ）という言葉は、スケールの第2番目のコードである、Ⅱmin7コードと、それに続く、スケール上の第5番目のコードである、ドミナントセブンスコードのことを意味します。ドミナントセブンスコードは、不安定で解決したいと思っていますから、ルート、換言すれば、スケールの1番目のコードに解決することになり、これでⅡⅤⅠ（ツーファイブワン）のサイクルが完結することになります。

Fメジャーのキーのダイアトニックセブンスコード

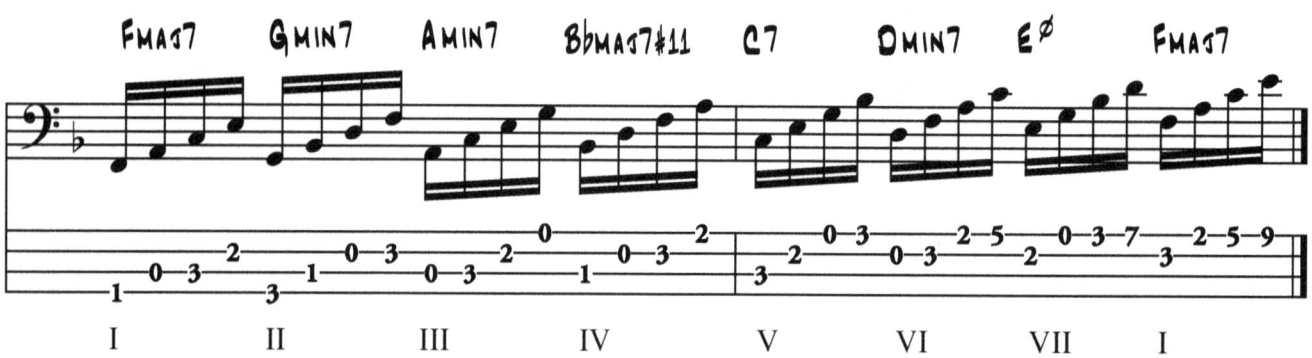

Fメジャーのキーにおいて、ベースラインにトライアドを用いた、ⅡⅤⅠ進行の例

Fメジャーのキーにおいて、ベースラインに音階的アプローチを用いた、ⅡⅤⅠ進行の例

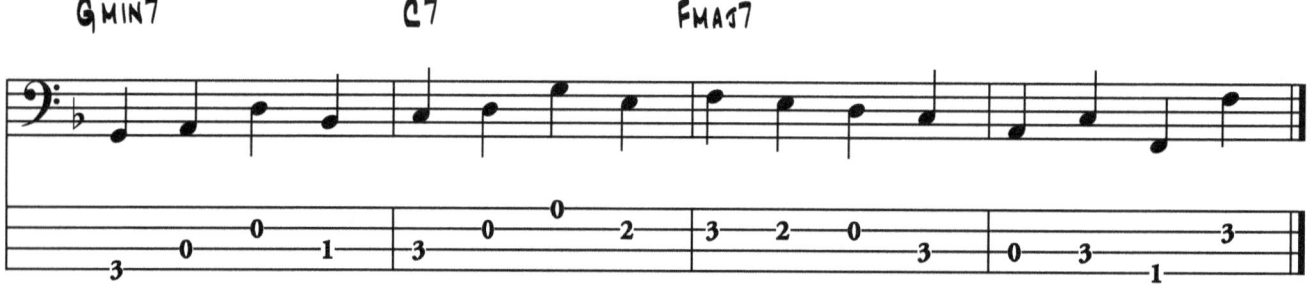

ジャズコード進行における II V I 進行の適用

次の例では、スタンダードコード進行の "Mr. K" において、"2"フィールを使った II V I 進行のベースラインを紹介しています。

最初のAセクションの、3，4小節目と7，8小節目に II V 進行があることに注目してください。2度目のAセクションでは、Bセクションの最初のコードである、B♭メジャーに繋がる II V 進行がみられます。

Aセクションでは、この II V 進行のベースラインに、3和音的アプローチを使っています。
Bセクション（ブリッジ）においては、音階的アプローチを使って書かれています。

©Waterfall Publishing House 2011

Standard Line Vol.I

Bセクションにおける音階的ベースライン例＝.....................

III VI II V 進行とフリジアンモード

下のチャートは、再度、Fメジャーのキーにおける、ダイアトニックセブンスコードの例になります。

このダイアトニックセブンスのチャートを見れば、III VI II V という進行の由来が分かるでしょう。次ページの例では、VIコードはドミナントセブンスコードとなっていますが、これはVIコードが、セカンダリードミナント*として機能しているからです。

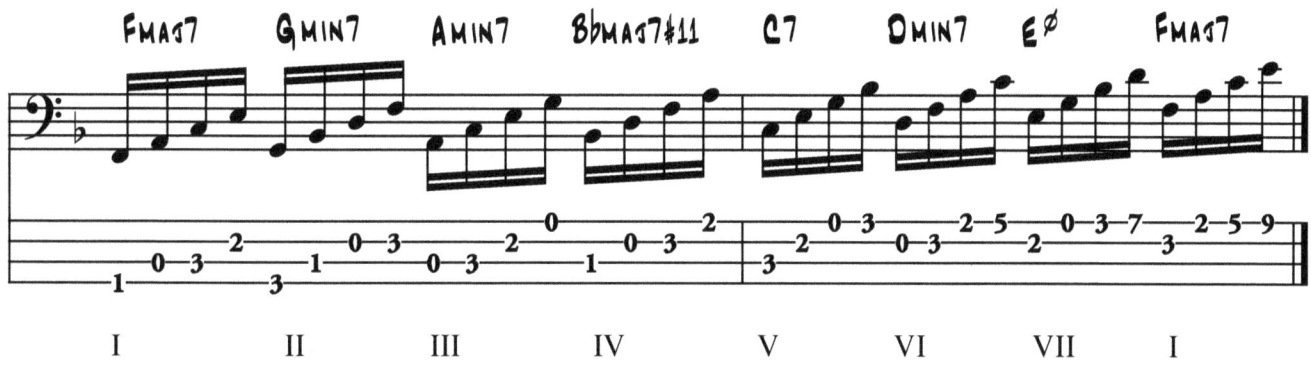

フリジアンモードまた III コード

Amin7　2オクターブのアルペジオ

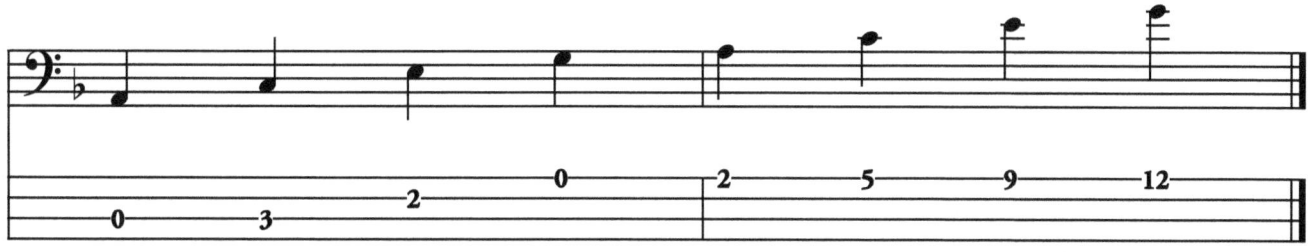

*セカンダリードミナントについては、Book II 及びBook IV にて詳しく解説しています。

Standard Line Vol.I

III VI II V 進行

続いて、ジャスのコード進行の中での、III VI II V 進行の機能について、見ていくことにします。
このIII VI II V の進行も、II V I 進行と同じように、ジャズスタンダードのレパートリーにおいて、最もよく使われる進行のひとつであり、12の全てのキーで学ぶ必要があります。

III VI II V とは、ダイアトニックセブンスコードのチャートの、三番目のコードであるIIImin7、六番目のコードであるVImin7またはサブスティチュートであるVI7、2番目のコードであるIImin7、そして、スケール上の5番目のコードであるV7のことを指します。ドミナントセブンスコードは解決しなくてはならないので、ルートであるIコードに戻ることになり、これにてIII VI II V I のサイクルが完結します。

トライアドを用いた、FメジャーのキーにおけるIII VI II V 進行の例

音階的アプローチを用いた、III VI II V 進行の例

©Waterfall Publishing House 2011

ジャズコード進行における III VI II V 進行の適用

次の例は、ジャズコード進行#4の "Mr. K" を示しています。

最初のAセクションの５小節から８小節にかけて、III VI II V の進行が見られます。最後のAセクションにおいては、５から６小節の２小節間に、III VI II V の進行が見られます。

セカンドAセクションの１、２小節目に注目すると、Fmaj7の三度の音程である、AからスタートしGmin7のルートであるGまで、Dmin7を挟みながら下降するAフリジアンスケールが見られます。
これはⅠコードを、III min7あるいはフリジアンスケールに置き換えることが出来るというサブスティチュートの例になります。

セカンドAセクションにおけるフリジアンモードベースライン例=....................

I VI II V 進行とエオリアンモード

次は、I VI II V の進行を見ていきます。この I VI II V の進行も、II V I 進行と同じように、ジャズのコード進行のボキャブラリーの中で、最も一般的なものの一つになります。下のダイアトニックセブンスのチャートより、I VI II V の由来が分かることと思います。

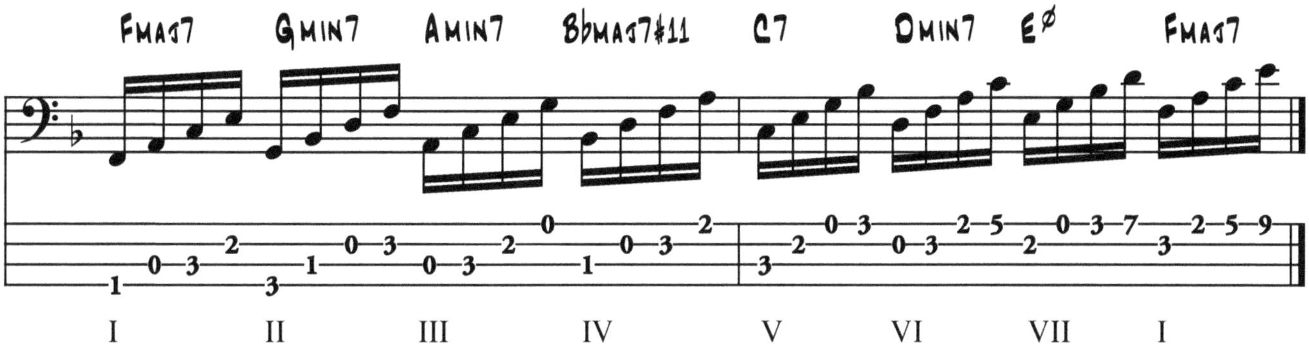

Dエオリアンスケール

Dmin7　2オクターブのアルペジオ

トライアドを用いた、FメジャーのキーにおけるI VI II V 進行の例

音階的アプローチを用いた、I VI II V 進行の例

I VI II V 進行における下降形ベースライン

トライアドを用いた、I VI II V 進行の例

音階的アプローチを用いた、I VI II V 進行の例になります。
モードを含む、音階的アプローチを用いることによって、ラインが何小節にも渡って、一方向に動くことが出来るということに注目してください。ここではAフリジアンスケールが、
Fmaj7コードに対して使われています。

"MR. K"

ジャズコード進行 #4

ジャズコード進行における I VI II V 進行の適用

Standard Line Vol.I

エオリアンモードベースラインもしくはそのバリエーション例＝......................

リディアンモード

リディアンモードはメジャースケール上の４番のモードであり、Maj7#11コードに対して使われます。

IVメジャーコードで曲が始まる場合や、ブリッジ（Bセクション）で、IVコードに転調したりするのは、機能的ジャズハーモニーにおいて、しばしば用いられる和声的手法のひとつです。

下のチャートはGメジャーのキーにおける、ダイアトニックセブンスを示しています。
このチャートを参照すれば、IVmaj7という言葉の由来が分かることと思います。

例1　２オクターブのCリディアンスケール

Cmaj7#11　２オクターブのアルペジオ

©Waterfall Publishing House 2011

Standard Line Vol.I

" IT DEPENDS "

ジャズコード進行＃5

ベースライン構築にリディアンモードを適用する

次のジャズコード進行 "IT DEPENDS" は IVメジャーコードで始まり、リディアンスケールの使用法を示しています。

©Waterfall Publishing House 2011

Standard Line Vol.I

Standard Line Vol.I

©Waterfall Publishing House 2011

Standard Line Vol.I

リディアンモードベースラインもしくはそのバリエーション例＝......................

ロクリアンモード

ロクリアンスケールとは、メジャースケール上の7番目のモードであり、ハーフディミニッシュドと呼ばれるmin7♭5に対して使われます。

下のチャートは、CメジャーのキーのダイアトニックセブンスをVII示しています。

チャートから、VIIハーフディミニッシュドがどこから来ているのかが分かるでしょう。

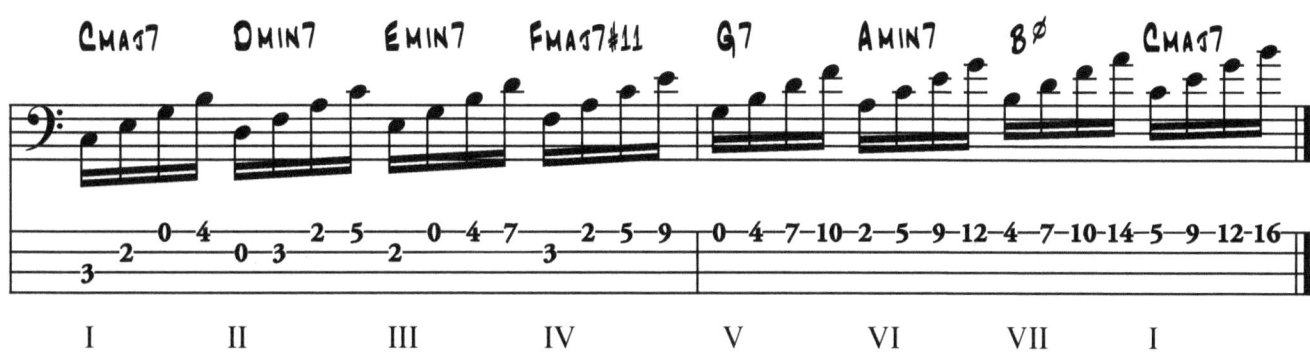

下の例は、VIIハーフディミニッシュドコード、またはCメジャースケール上の7番目のモードである、ロクリアンスケールを表しています。

例1　2オクターブのBロクリアンスケール

例2　2オクターブのBmin7♭5アルペジオ

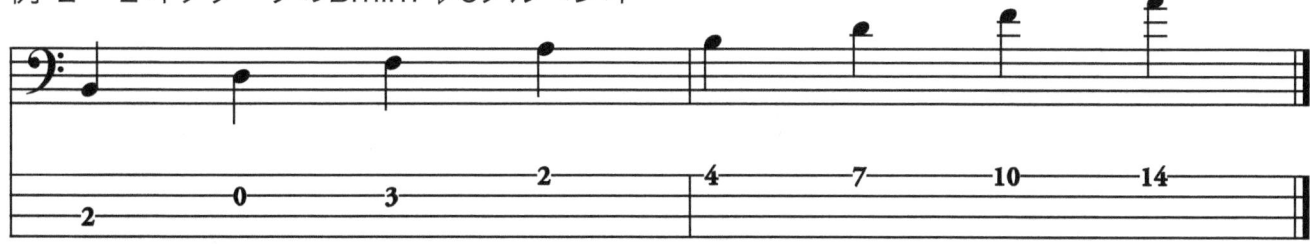

次のジャズコード進行 "THE WEAVING STREAM" では、大きく分けたAセクションとBセクションの各3小節目で、VIIハーフディミニッシュドコード及びロクリアンモードが実際に使用されています。

©Waterfall Publishing House 2011

Standard Line Vol.I

" THE WEAVING STREAM " ジャズコード進行 #6
ベースライン構築にロクリアンモードを適用する

Standard Line Vol.I

©Waterfall Publishing House 2011

73

Standard Line Vol.I

ロクリアンモードベースラインもしくはそのバリエーション例＝……………………

パート２　　　シンメトリック、メロディックマイナースケール

この本のパート２では、スタンダードジャズレパートリーにおいて、ベースラインを作っていく時に使われる、シンメトリック（音程に均整のとれた）スケール、及びメロディックマイナースケールからのモードの使用について、説明していきます。

これまでは、メジャースケールから派生する、スケールとモードについて見てきました。

この本の次のセクションでは、シンメトリックスケールとして知られるスケールについて見ていきます。

ホールトーンスケール

ディミニッシュドスケール（全音、半音）

ディミニッシュドスケール（半音、全音）

メロディックマイナースケールから派生し、マイナーⅡⅤⅠ進行に使われるスケールについても同様に見ていきます。

オルタードスケール

ロクリアン#2スケール

メロディックマイナースケール（ジャズにおける）

このチャプターでは、ジャズのボキャブラリーでよく使われる、上昇するメロディックマイナースケールについて説明していきます。
クラシック音楽においては、メロディックマイナースケールは、下降する際には、6thと7thが♭する少し違った形になります。

ホールトーンスケール

ホールトーンスケールはシンメトリックスケールのひとつです。すなわち、スケール内の音程が、一貫したパターンを持っているということです。ここではホールトーンスケールの名前の所為である全音程（ホールトーン）のことになります。

この６音で構成されるホールトーンスケールは、独特のサウンドを持っていて、Dom7#5コードや、Dom7♭5コードに対してしばしば使われます。この全音程のスケールの構造上、実際には２つのホールトーンスケールしか存在せず、その他のホールトーンスケールは、始まる音が異なるのみで、その２つのスケールが基になっています。次のAABAの形式のコード進行で、Aセクションの３、４小節目のD7♭5コードに対して、ホールトーンスケールが使用されています。

例１　Dホールトーンスケール

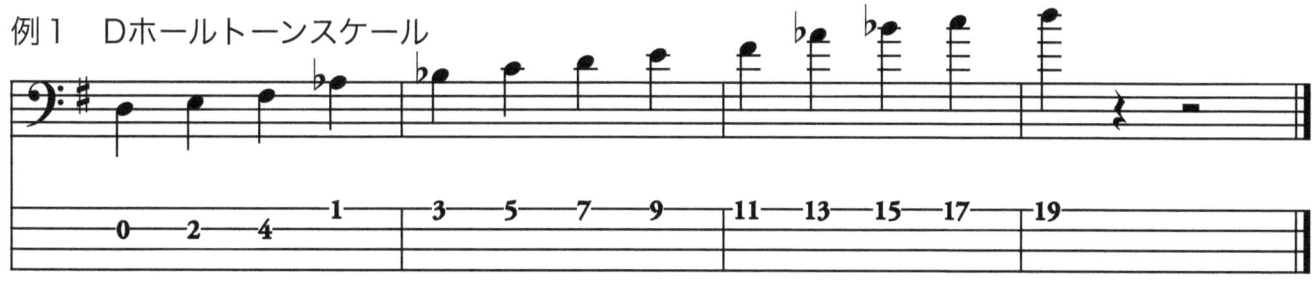

例２　D7♯5 ２オクターブのアルペジオ

" WHERES THE SUBWAY "　　ジャズコード進行＃７
ジャズベースラインにホールトーンスケールを適用する

©Waterfall Publishing House 2011

Standard Line Vol.I

Standard Line Vol.I

©Waterfall Publishing House 2011

Standard Line Vol.I

©Waterfall Publishing House 2011

Standard Line Vol.1

ホールトーンスケールベースラインもしくはそのバリエーション例＝......................

ディミニッシュドスケール

ディミニッシュドスケールは、8音からなる、もう一つのシンメトリックスケールで、全音、半音の音程の並びになっています。ディミニッシュドスケールは、Dim7コードにおいて使われます。
その均整のとれた音程の並びにより、実際には3つのディミニッシュドスケールしか存在しません。

例1　2オクターブのA♭ディミニッシュドスケール

2オクターブのA♭ディミニッシュドアルペジオ

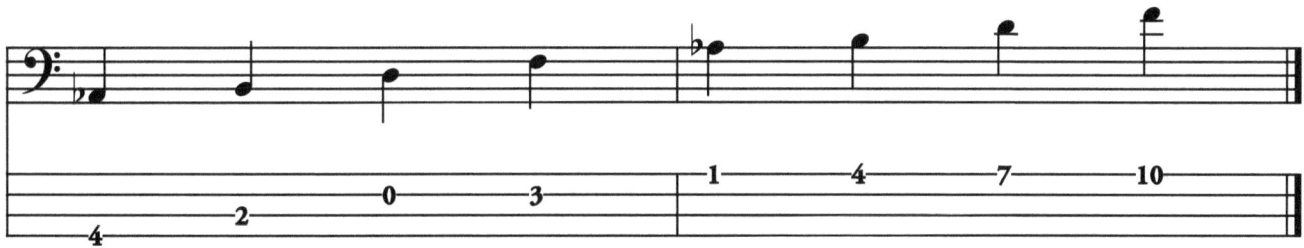

短3度毎に、全音、半音の順番でスケールを組み立てて見ると、同じスケールから、4つのディミニッシュドスケールが出来るということがわかると思います。A♭、B、D、Fディミニッシュドスケールは、異なった音から始まるというだけで、同じスケールです。

A♭から半音上がって、ディミニッシュドスケールを組み立てることによって、A、C、E♭、G♭ディミニッシュドスケールが出来ます。

同じくAから半音上げて、このスケールを作ると、B♭、D♭、E、Gディミニッシュドスケールが出来ます。

次の例は、Aディミニッシュドスケールを表しています。

Standard Line Vol.I

次の例は、B♭ディミニッシュドスケールを表しています

次のジャズコード進行"FINDING CANDY"では、最初と2度目の、前半部の2小節目と6小節目で、ディミニッシュドスケールが使われています。

"FINDING CANDY"　　　　ジャズコード進行＃8

ジャズベースラインにおけるディミニッシュドスケールの適用

©Waterfall Publishing House 2011

Standard Line Vol.I

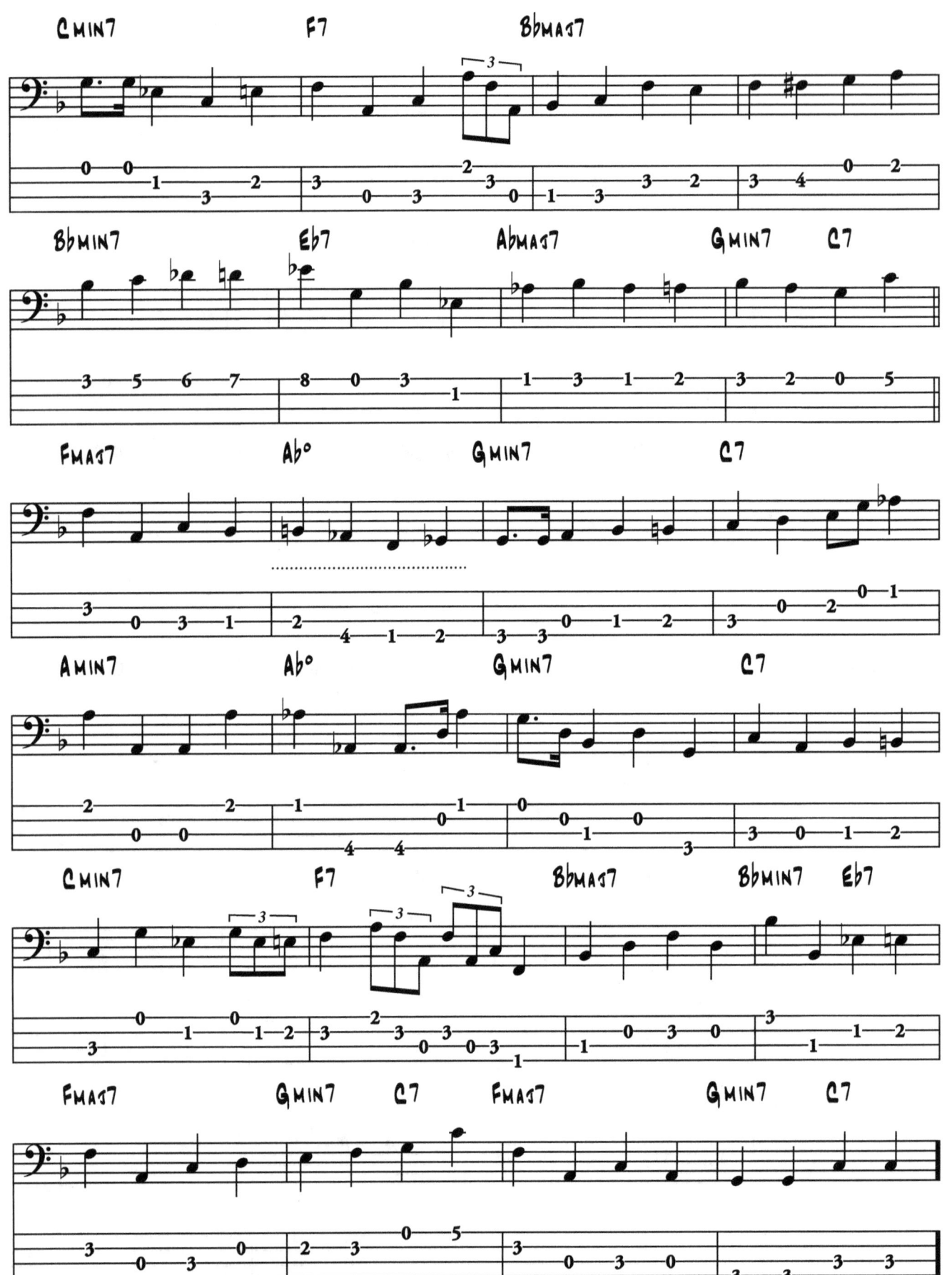

©Waterfall Publishing House 2011

Standard Line Vol.I

ディミニッシュドスケールベースラインもしくはそのバリエーション例＝......................

ハーフホールディミニッシュドスケール

　ハーフホールディミニッシュドスケールは、半音、全音のパターンの音程を持ち、8音からなるシンメトリックスケールの一つです。
　このハーフホールディミニッシュドスケールは、ドミナントセブンス♭9コード上でしばしば使われます。均整のとれた音程により、このハーフホールディミニッシュドスケールは3つしか存在しません。
　下の例は、Cハーフホールディミニッシュドスケールを表しています。
　またこのCハーフホールディミニッシュドスケールは、B♭ディミニッシュドスケール（全音、半音パターンの）と同じであることがわかります。

Cハーフホールディミニッシュドスケール

2オクターブのC7♭9アルペジオ

短3度毎に、半音、全音の音程でスケールを組み立てると、同じスケールから、4つのハーフホールディミニッシュドスケールが出来ます。A♭、B、D、Fハーフホールディミニッシュドスケールは、異なった音から始まる、同じスケールです。

A♭から半音上げて、このスケールを作ると、A、C、E♭、G♭のハーフホールディミニッシュドスケールができます。

Aから半音上げて、このスケールを作ると、B♭、D♭、E、Gハーフホールディミニッシュドスケールができます。

次の例はAハーフホールディミニッシュドスケールを表しています

次の例はB♭ハーフホールディミニッシュドスケールを表しています

次のジャズコード進行 "VEGETABLE STEW"は4つの8小節、ＡＢＣＤで成り立っています。
ハーフホールディミニッシュドスケールは、ＡＢとDセクションの2小節目のC7♭9コードにおいて使われています。

" VEGETABLE STEW "　　　　ジャズコード進行＃9

ジャズベースラインにおけるハーフホールディミニッシュドスケールの適用

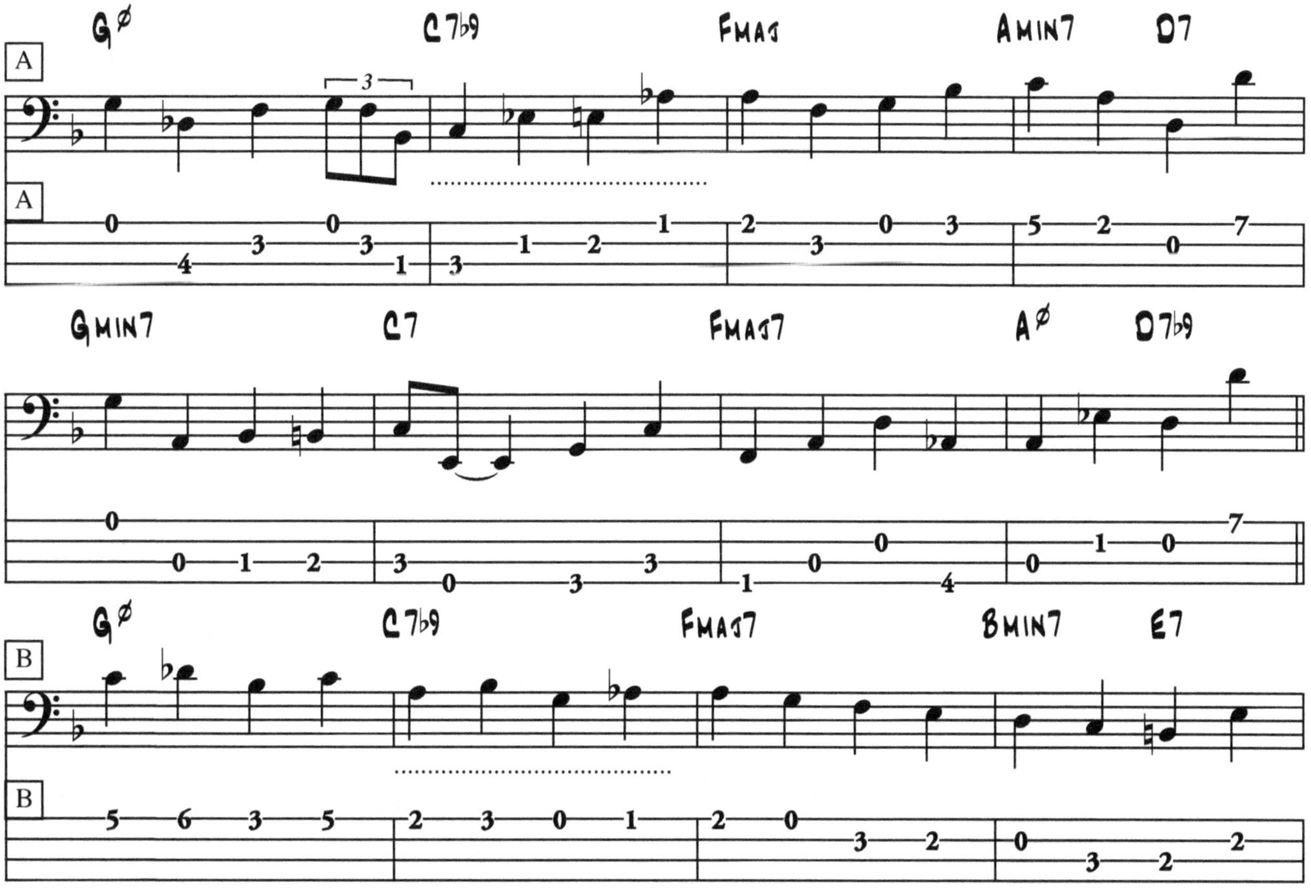

Standard Line Vol.I

Standard Line Vol.I

©Waterfall Publishing House 2011

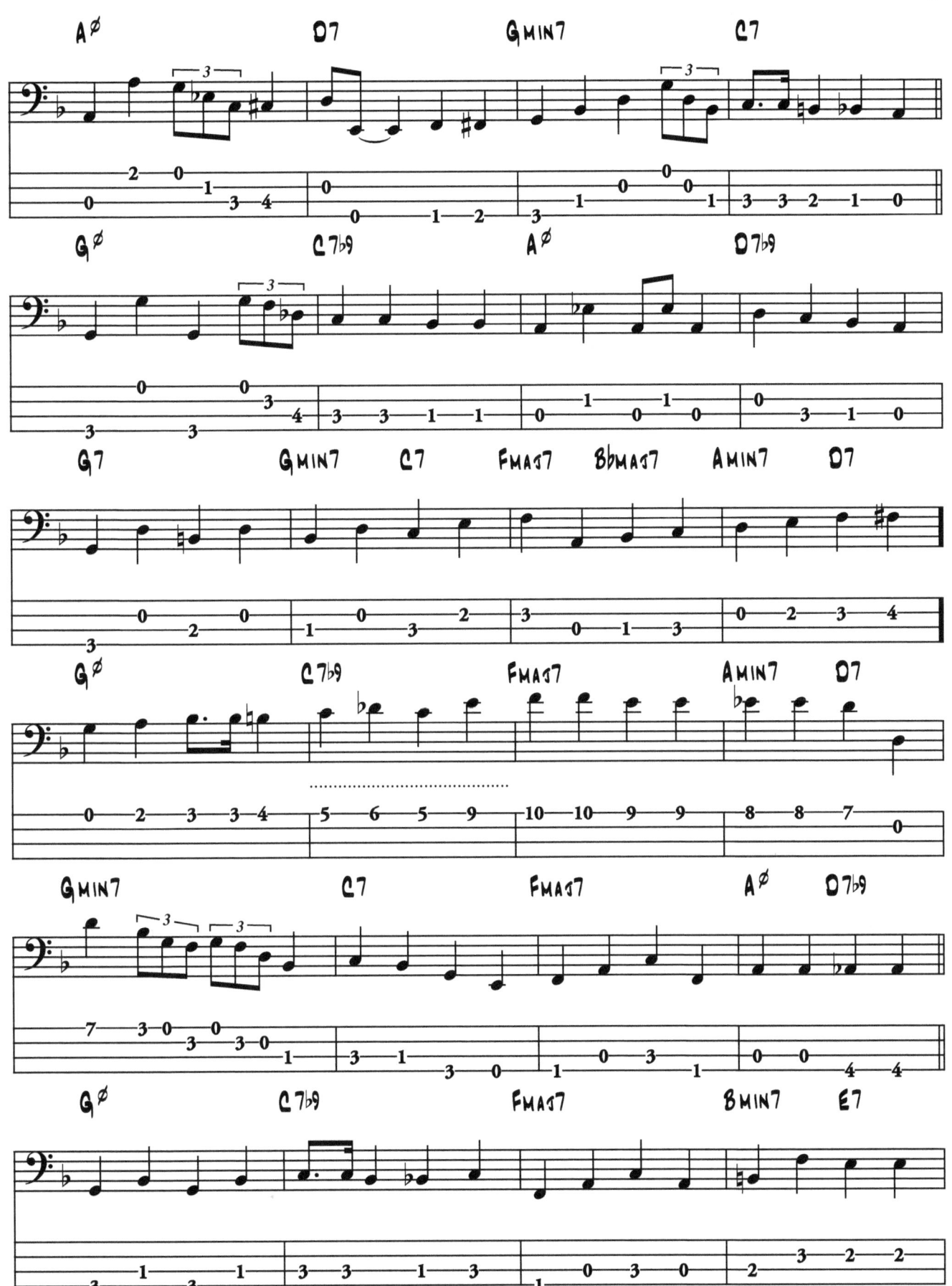

Standard Line Vol.I

ハーフホールディミニッシュドスケールベースラインもしくはそのバリエーション例＝......................

ディミニッシュドホールトーンスケールと、マイナー II V 進行

ディミニッシュドホールトーンスケールは、メロディックマイナースケールの7番目のモードであり、オルタードセブンスコードにおいて使われます。

このスケールは、ディミニッシュドスケールのように始まり、ホールトーンスケールのように終わることから、この名が付いています。

ディミニッシュドホールトーンスケールは、マイナー II V I 進行で、V コードのような機能を持ちます。

例 1　B♭メロディックマイナースケール*

例 2　2オクターブのAディミニッシュドホールトーンスケール

例 3　2オクターブのAオルタードアルペジオ

*メロディックマイナースケールは、長7度を用いて作られています。このスケールは、長3度の代わりに短3度を用いたメジャースケールのようでもあります。

Standard Line Vol.I   "MOONLIGHT VIEW"   ジャズコード進行 #10

ジャズベースラインにおける、ディミニッシュドホールトーンスケールの適用

Standard Line Vol.I

©Waterfall Publishing House 2011

Standard Line Vol.I

ディミニッシュドホールトーンスケールベースラインもしくはそのバリエーション例＝......................

ロクリアン♯2モードとマイナーⅡⅤ進行

ロクリアン♯2(シャープツー) スケールは、メロディックマイナーの6番目のモードであり、min7♭5コード上で使われ、マイナーⅡⅤ進行のⅡコードとして機能します。

例 1　Gメロディックマイナースケール

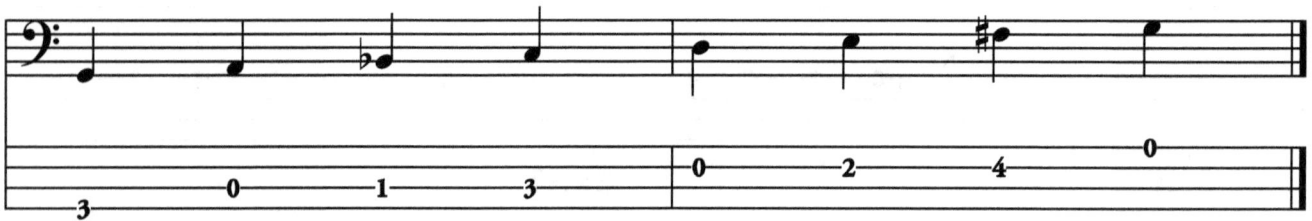

例 2　Eロクリアン♯2スケール

例 3　Emin7♭5アルペジオ

©Waterfall Publishing House 2011

" MOONLIGHT VIEW "

ジャズコード進行 #10

ジャズベースラインにおけるロクリアン♯2の適用

Standard Line Vol.I

Standard Line Vol.I

ロクリアン♯２モードスケールベースラインもしくはそのバリエーション例＝......................

Standard Line Vol.I

マイナー II V 進行

いくつかの例でマイナー II V I 進行を見てきましたが、次の例では、メジャーキーにおける II V I 進行との違いについて見ていくことにします。

メジャーキーにおける II V I では、ウォーキングベースラインを組み立てる上で、ドリアン、ミクソリディアンスケールをそれぞれ使用します。コード進行のキーは変わりません。

マイナー II V I 進行では、ロクリアン♯２スケールおよびディミニッシュドホールトーンスケールをそれぞれ II と V において使用します。
違いとは、このマイナー II V I 進行を形作る、ロクリアン♯２とディミニッシュドホールトーンスケールはそれぞれ異なったキーから来ていることです。

ＣメジャーのII V Iを例として下に示します。

Ｃメジャーにおける II V I 進行では、Dドリアンスケール、Gミクソリディアンスケールをそれぞれ、II と V に使用し、Cメジャースケールに戻ります。全てのスケールは、Cメジャースケールに由来するモードであり、4小節中ずっとCメジャーと言えます。

次の例は、CマイナーのキーのマイナーII V進行を表しています。

この例では、マイナー II V I は、3つのキーを移動します。Dmin7♭5コードは、Fメロディックマイナースケールの6番目のモードです。
Gオルタードコードは、A♭メロディックマイナーの7番目のモードです。
CminM7コードはIコード、或はCメロディックマイナースケールのトニックマイナーということです。

©Waterfall Publishing House 2011

下の例では、マイナーⅡⅤⅠ進行で使われるコードスケールと、その関係するキーを示しています。

例 1　Fメロディックマイナースケール

Cマイナーの、マイナーⅡⅤⅠのⅡコードで使用されるDロクリアン♯2スケール

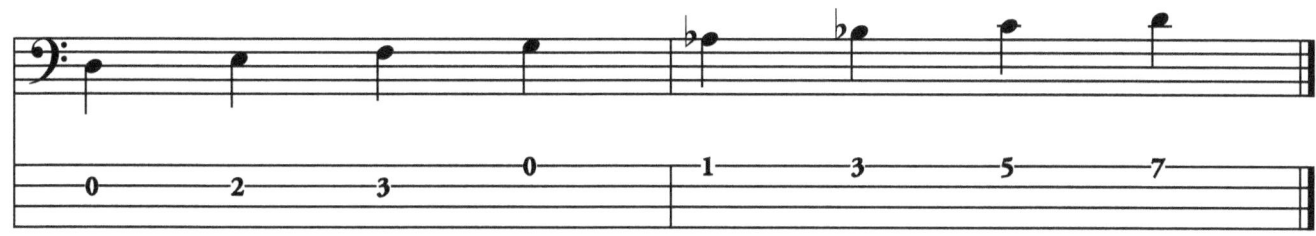

例 2　A♭メロディックマイナースケール

CマイナーのⅡⅤⅠのⅤコードで使われるGオルタードスケール（ディミニッシュドホールトーンスケール）

Standard Line Vol.I

例 3　Cメロディックマイナースケール

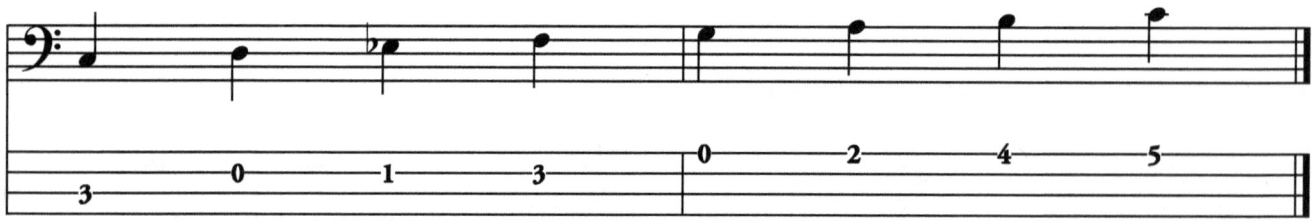

CマイナーのマイナーⅡⅤⅠのⅠコードとして使われる、CマイナーメジャーセブンススケールCマイナーメジャーセブンススケール、またはトニックマイナー

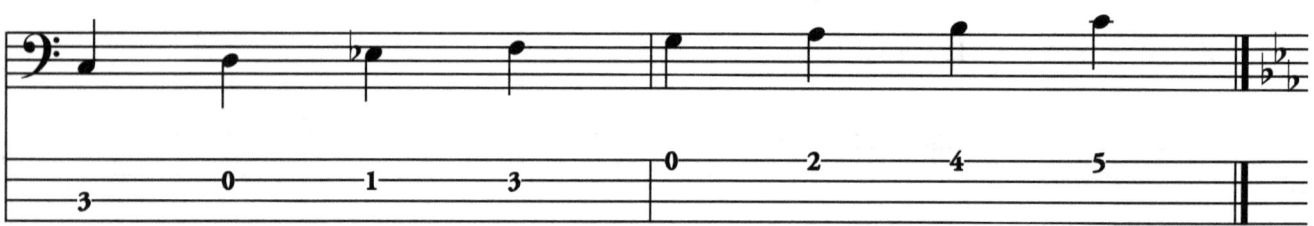

©Waterfall Publishing House 2011

パートIII　　　　　　　　　ビバップスケール

上昇するメジャービバップスケール

ビバップスケールとは、ウォーキングベースラインやインプロビゼーションにおいて、そのラインに、前に進む動きを与える追加的な経過音を含むスケールのことを言います。
クロマティックパッシングトーン（経過的半音）は同じスケールを使って、より長いラインでハーモニーを輪郭づけるのに役立ちます。

例1では、2オクターブの上昇するE♭メジャースケールを表しています。

3小節目の一拍目、ダウンビートであるこの小節の最初の拍はFになっていて、次にくるダウンビート、すなわち3小節目の3拍目はA♭であり、これはE♭メジャースケールにおけるアボイドノートとなっていることに注目してください。

この3小節目から示されているものは、E♭メジャーではなく、Fマイナーのように見えます。

アボイドノートとは何でしょう？　アボイドノートとは、ここではメジャーコード（ⅠMajor）に対して、ダウンビートで使わないように、とされているメジャースケールにおける4番目の音（コードトーンの第3音に半音でぶつかる為）のことを言います。

例1　2オクターブのE♭メジャースケール。1拍目と3拍目がダウンビートです。

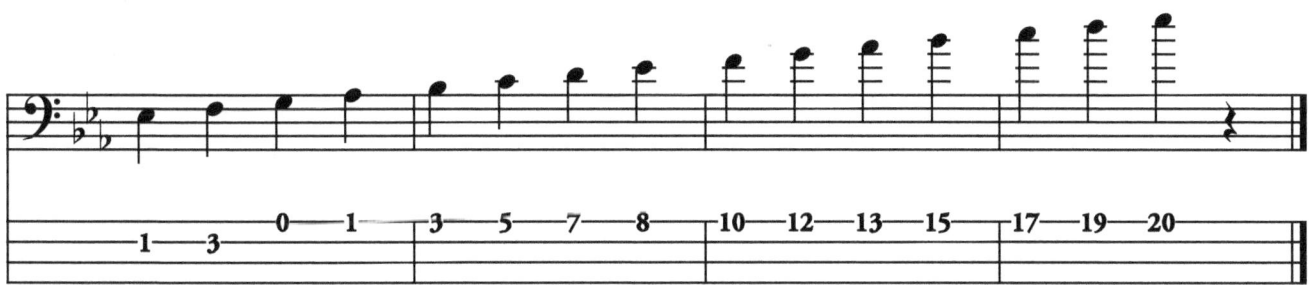

次の例2は、2オクターブにわたるE♭メジャービバップスケールになります。
ここでは、クロマティックパッシングトーンであるB音、またはスケールの♭6thが加わることによって、より長いラインにおいて力強く前に進む動きが生まれます。
これで全てのダウンビートはコードトーンを含むことになり、はっきりとハーモニーの輪郭が感じられ、ラインがどこに向かって進むのかという感覚も得られます。

例2　2オクターブのE♭メジャービバップスケール。1拍目と3拍目がダウンビートです。

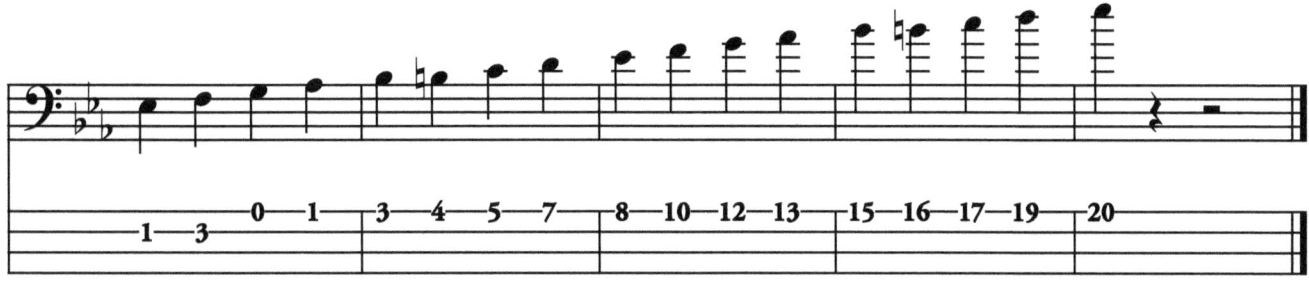

©Waterfall Publishing House 2011

Standard Line Vol.I

下降するメジャービバップスケール

例3は、2オクターブにわたって下降するE♭メジャースケールを示しています。

3小節目の一拍目、すなわちダウンビートはDで、次のダウンビートである3拍目はB♭になっています。

ここで示されているものは、B♭7あるいはDハーフディミニッシュであると言えるでしょう。

例3　2オクターブの下降するE♭メジャースケール。1拍目と3拍目がダウンビートです。

例4では、2オクターブにわたるE♭メジャービバップスケール（下降形）になります。
ここでは、クロマティックパッシングトーンであるB音、またはスケールの♭6thが加わることによって、より長いラインにおいて力強く前に進む動きが生まれています。
これで全てのダウンビートはコードトーンを含むことになり、はっきりとハーモニーの輪郭が感じられ、ラインがどこに向かって進むのかという感覚も得られます。
1小節目と3小節目の、1拍目と3拍目が、E♭とCになっています。これはE♭メジャーシックスのサウンドで、この4小節中のダウンビートは、E♭、C、B♭、GとなっていてE♭メジャーの調性をよく示していると言えるでしょう。

例4　2オクターブのE♭メジャービバップスケール（下降形）。1拍目と3拍目がダウンビートです。

次の例は、ジャズコード進行#11の "MORE STEW?" を見ていく中で、メジャービバップスケールをベースラインに適用していきます。

＊このE♭は、通常のチューニングのダブルベース、あるいは4弦エレクトリックベースでは、音域外の音で、このトピックの説明のために使われています。5弦ベース、C Extensionを付けたダブルベースでは弾くことができます。

©Waterfall Publishing House 2011

" MORE STEW ? " ジャズコード進行 # 11

ジャズベースラインにおけるメジャービバップスケールの適用

Standard Line Vol.I

Standard Line Vol.I

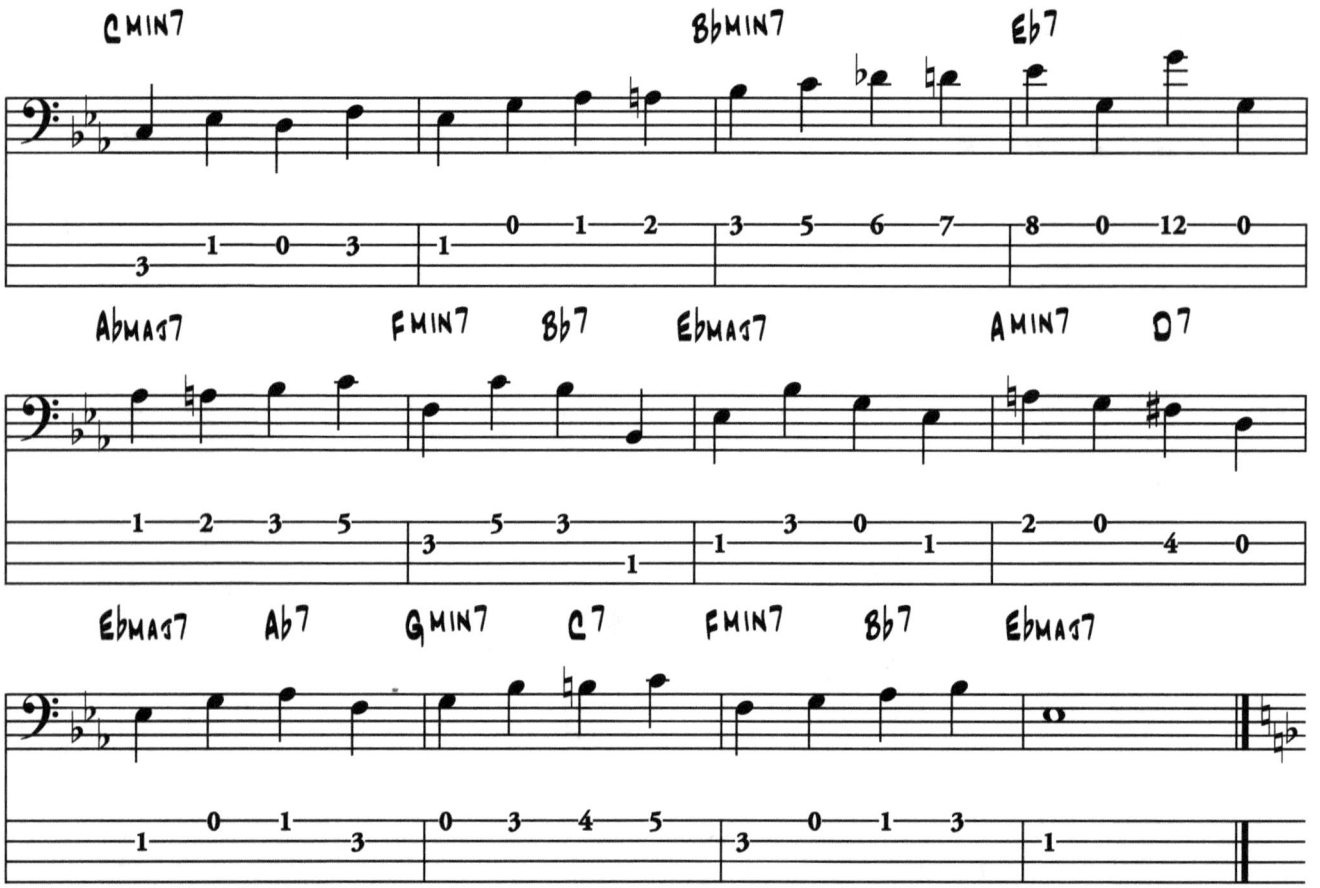

メジャービバップスケールベースラインもしくはそのバリエーション例＝......................

上昇するドリアンマイナービバップスケール

ビバップスケールのドリアンモードに対する適用について見ていきます。

例1は、2オクターブのGドリアンスケールを表しています。

3小節目の1拍目、ダウンビートはAであり、次のダウンビートである3拍目はCになっています。

3小節目から示されているものはAマイナーになっていると言えます。

例1　2オクターブのGドリアンスケール。1拍目と3拍目がダウンビートです。

例2では、2オクターブのGドリアンマイナービバップスケール（上昇形）が示されています。クロマティックパッシングトーンであるF#音、またはスケールのメジャー7thが加わることによって、より長いラインにおいて力強く前に進む動きが生まれています。
全てのダウンビートはコードトーンを含むことになり、はっきりとハーモニーの輪郭が感じられ、ラインがどこに向かって進むのかという感覚も得られます。

例2　2オクターブのGドリアンマイナービバップスケール。1拍目と3拍目がダウンビートです。

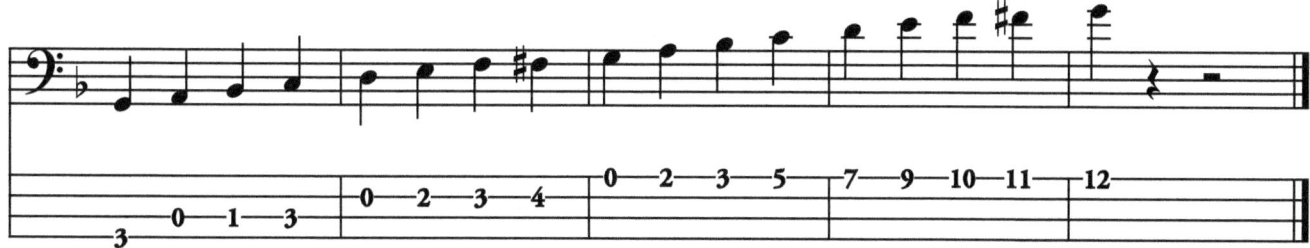

Standard Line Vol.I

下降するドリアンマイナービバップスケール

例 3は、2オクターブにわたり、下降するGドリアンスケールを表しています。

3小節目の1拍目、ダウンビートがFで、次のダウンビートはDになっています。

3小節目はDmin7になってしまっています。

例 3　2オクターブの下降するGドリアンスケール。1拍目と3拍目がダウンビートです。

例 4では、2オクターブのGドリアンマイナービバップスケール（下降形）が示されています。これまでに述べたことと同様に、クロマティックパッシングトーン F#(スケールのメジャー7th) が加わることによって、ダウンビートがコードトーンになることで、ハーモニーの輪郭や、ラインの方向性、調性が明快になります。この4小節中のダウンビートは、G , F , D , Bbとなっていて Gmin7 の調性をよく示していると言えるでしょう。

例 4　2オクターブのGドリアンマイナービバップスケール（下降形）1拍目と3拍目がダウンビートです。

次の例では、ジャズコード進行#12の "HEARD IT" を見ていく中で、ドリアンマイナービバップスケールをベースラインに適用していきます。

©Waterfall Publishing House 2011

"HEARD IT"

ジャズコード進行 #12

ジャズベースラインにおけるドリアンマイナービバップスケールの適用

Standard Line Vol.I

©Waterfall Publishing House 2011

Standard Line Vol.I

©Waterfall Publishing House 2011

Standard Line Vol.I

©Waterfall Publishing House 2011

ドリアンマイナービバップスケールベースラインもしくはそのバリエーション例＝……………

Standard Line Vol.I

ミクソリディアンビバップスケール

上昇するミクソリディアンビバップスケール

ドミナントセブンスビバップスケールは、ミクソリディアンスケールの♭7thとルートの間にクロマティックパッシングトーンを加えたものです。下の例の、F7ビバップスケールでは、クロマティックパッシングトーンはE、スケールのメジャー7thになります。

例1は2オクターブの上昇するミクソリディアンスケールを示しています。
3小節目の1拍目、ダウンビートがG、次のダウンビートはB♭になっていて、これでは実際に示されているのはGmin7ということになります。

例1　2オクターブのF7ミクソリディアンスケール。1拍目と3拍目がダウンビートになります。

次の例2は、2オクターブにわたるFミクソリディアンビバップスケールになります。

他の例と同様に、クロマティックパッシングトーンEが加わることにより、ダウンビートがコードトーンになることで、ハーモニーの輪郭や、ラインの方向性が明確になります。

例2　2オクターブのFミクソリディアンビバップスケール（上昇形）。1拍目と3拍目がダウンビートです。

©Waterfall Publishing House 2011

下降するミクソリディアンビバップスケール

例3は、下降する2オクターブのFミクソリディアンスケールを示しています。

3小節目のダウンビートである1拍と3拍が、それぞれE♭とCになっています。

3小節目はE♭6、あるいはCmin7のようにきこえてしまいます。

例3　2オクターブのFミクソリディアンスケール。1拍目と3拍目がダウンビートです。

例4では、2オクターブのFミクソリディアンスケール（下降形）が示されています。
他の例と同様に、クロマティックパッシングトーンEが加わることで、3小節目のダウンビートがコードトーンになり、ハーモニーの輪郭、ラインの方向性が明確になり、3，4小節目のダウンビートが、それぞれF、E♭、C、Aとなり、F7としての調性も明らかです。

例4　2オクターブのFミクソリディアンビバップスケール（下降形）。1拍目と3拍目がダウンビートです。

次の例では、ジャズコード進行#13の"WHO'S GLOVE"を見ていく中で、ミクソリディアンビバップスケールをベースラインに適用していきます。

©Waterfall Publishing House 2011

Standard Line Vol.1

"WHO'S GLOVE ?" ジャズコード進行 #13

ベースラインにミクソリディアンビバップスケールを適用する

©Waterfall Publishing House 2011

Standard Line Vol.I

Standard Line Vol.I

©Waterfall Publishing House 2011

ミクソリディアンビバップスケールベースラインもしくはそのバリエーション例＝……………

Standard Line Vol.I

©Waterfall Publishing House 2011

パートIV　スタンダードジャズコード進行のベースライン例

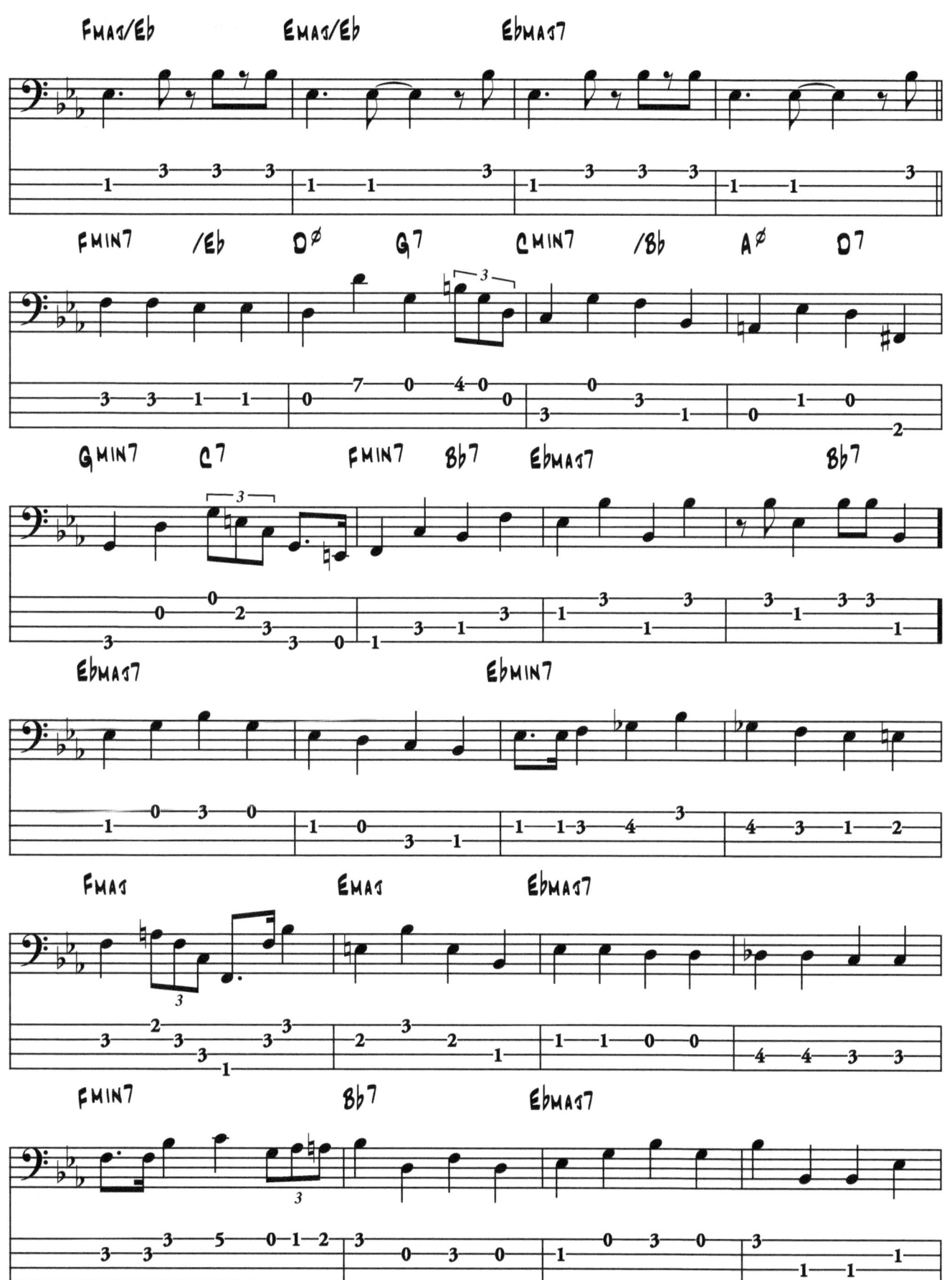

Standard Line Vol.I

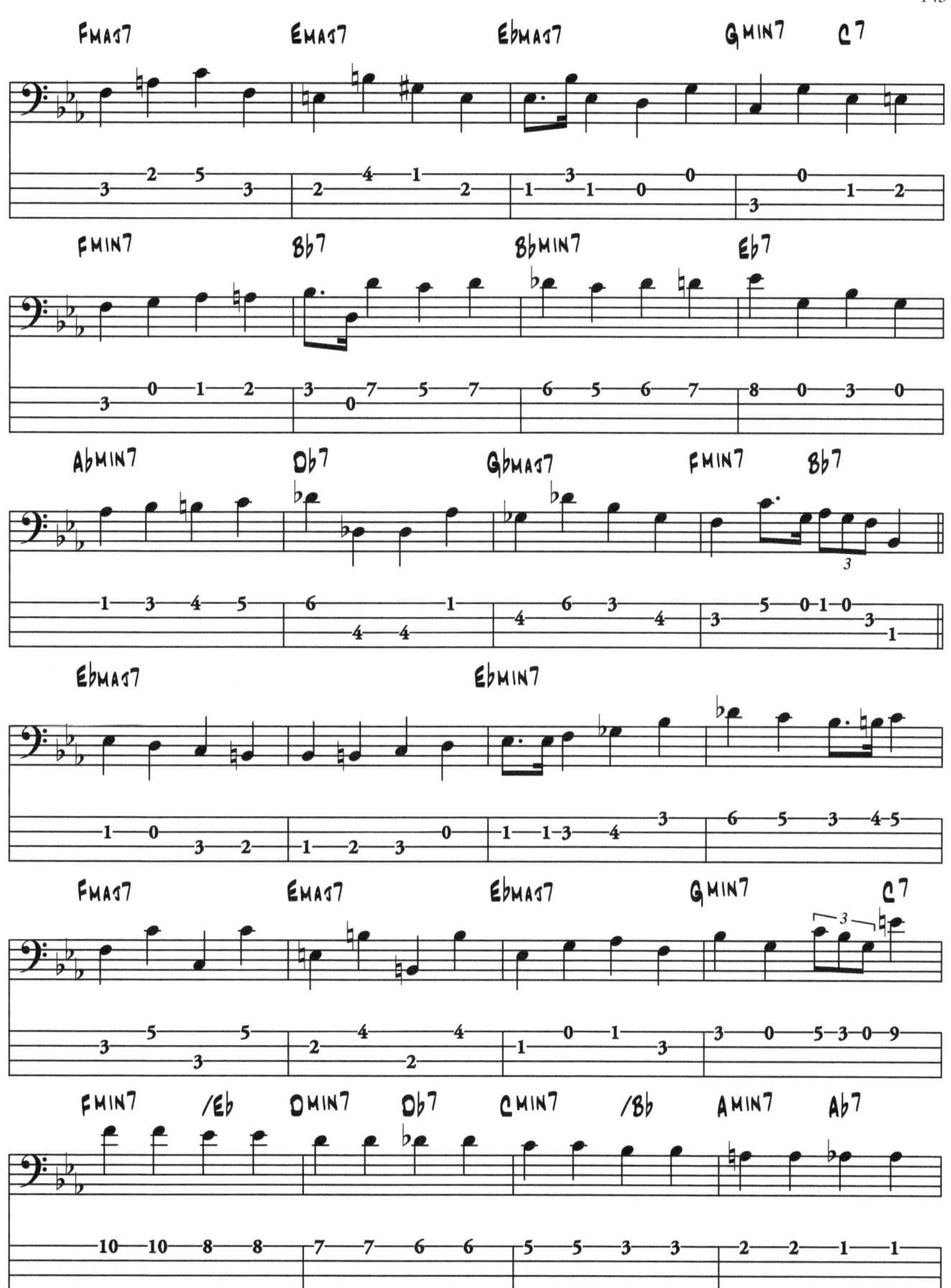

Standard Line Vol.I

Standard Line Vol.I

"SLIPPED INTO THE STREAM"   ジャズコード進行 #15

Standard Line Vol.I

Standard Line Vol.I

Standard Line Vol.I

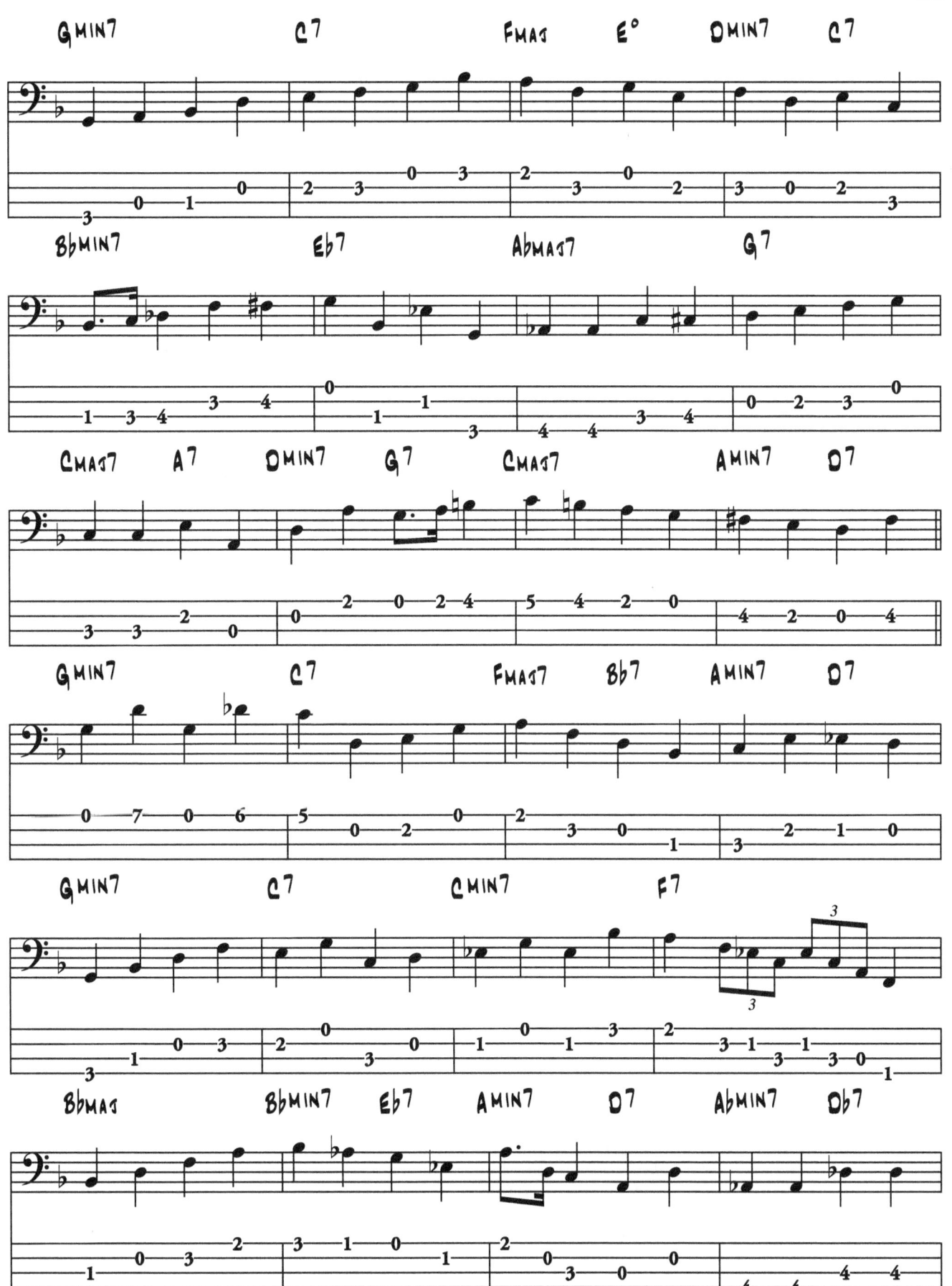

Standard Line Vol.I

Standard Line Vol.I

" THE ONE IN GLOVES "

ジャズコード進行 #17

©Waterfall Publishing House 2011

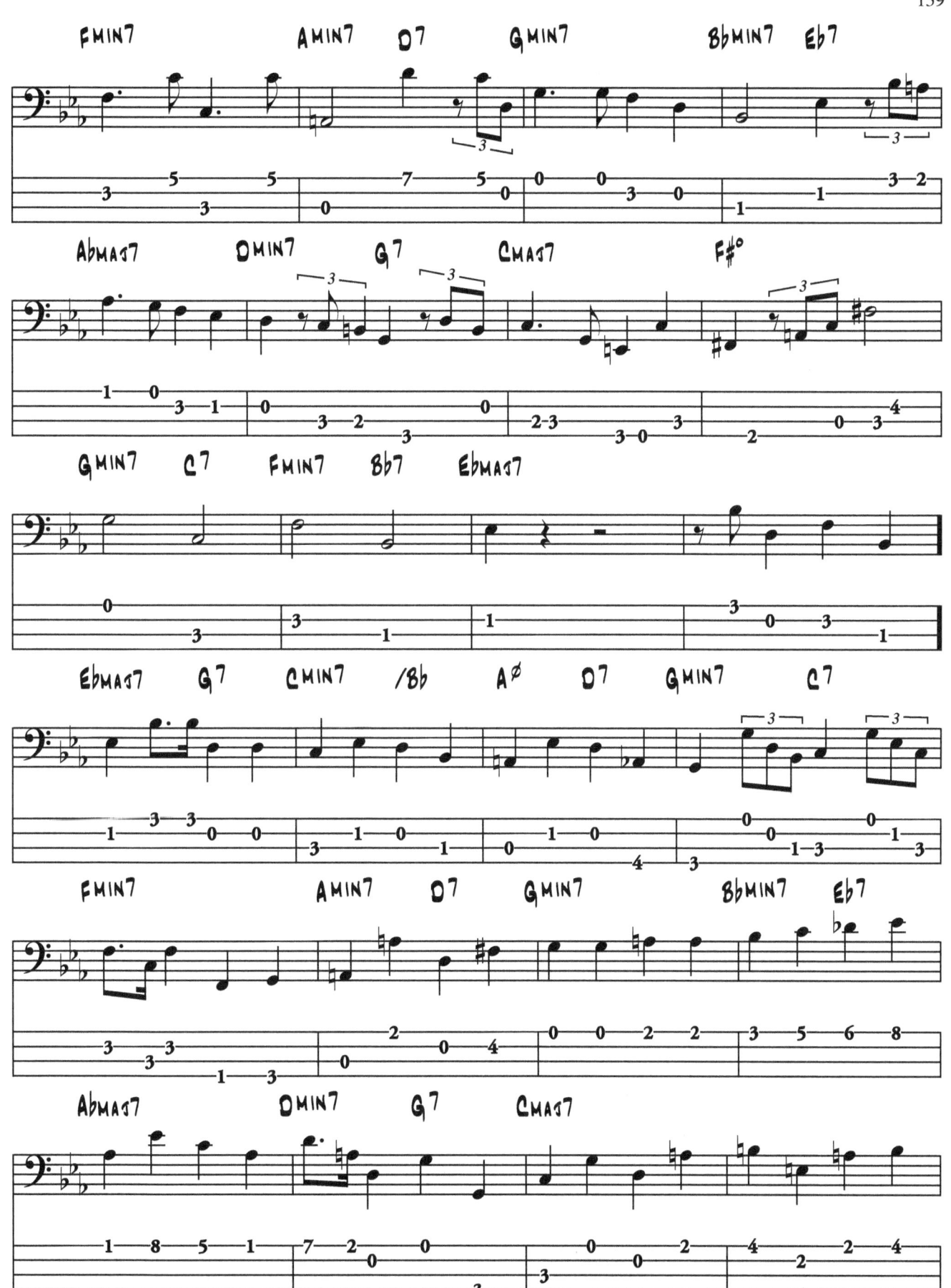

Standard Line Vol.I

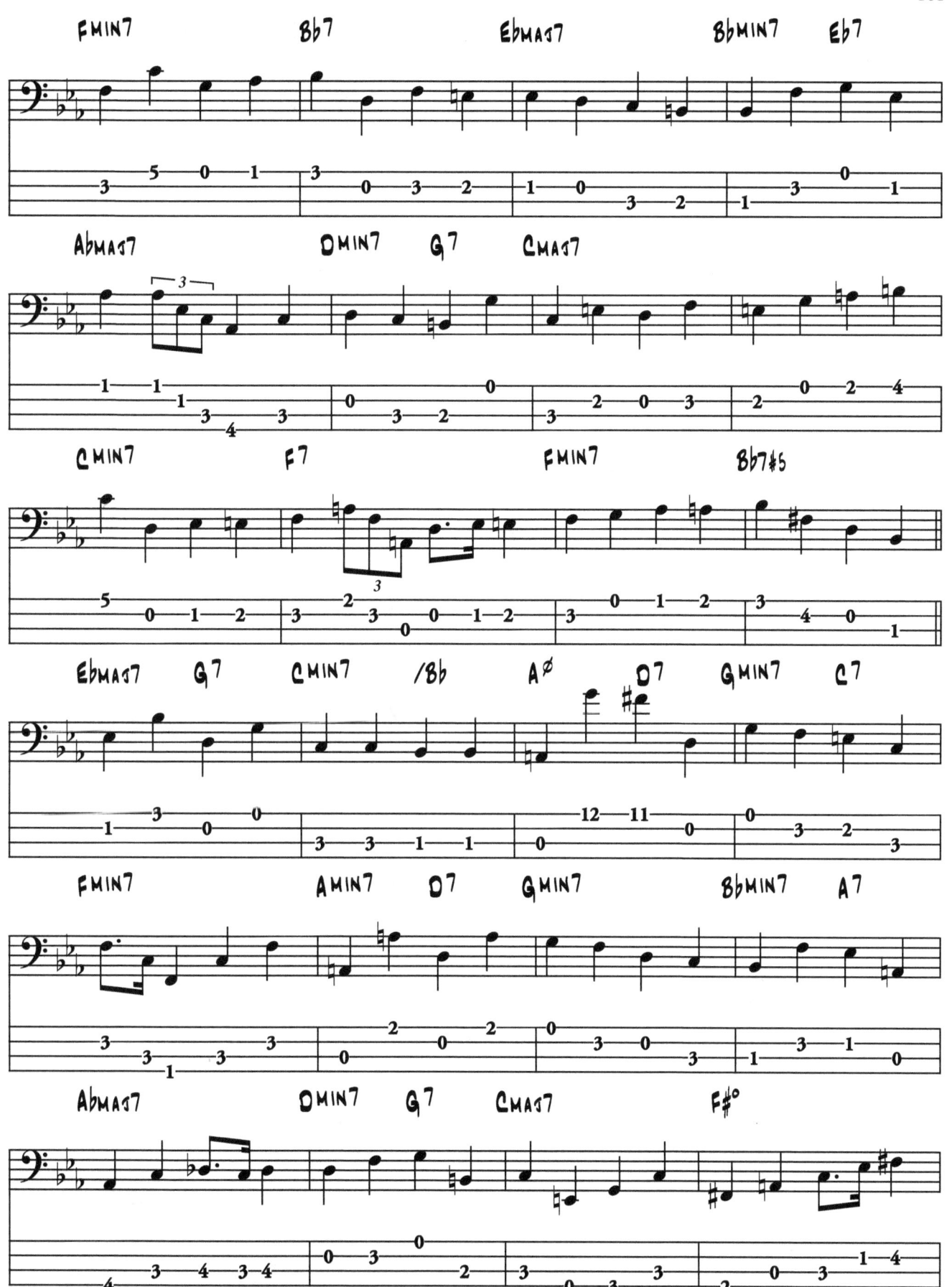

Standard Line Vol.I

Standard Line Vol.I

"GARDEN HOSES"

ジャズコード進行 #18

Standard Line Vol.I

©Waterfall Publishing House 2011

Standard Line Vol.I

Standard Line Vol.I

Standard Line Vol.I

Standard Line Vol.I

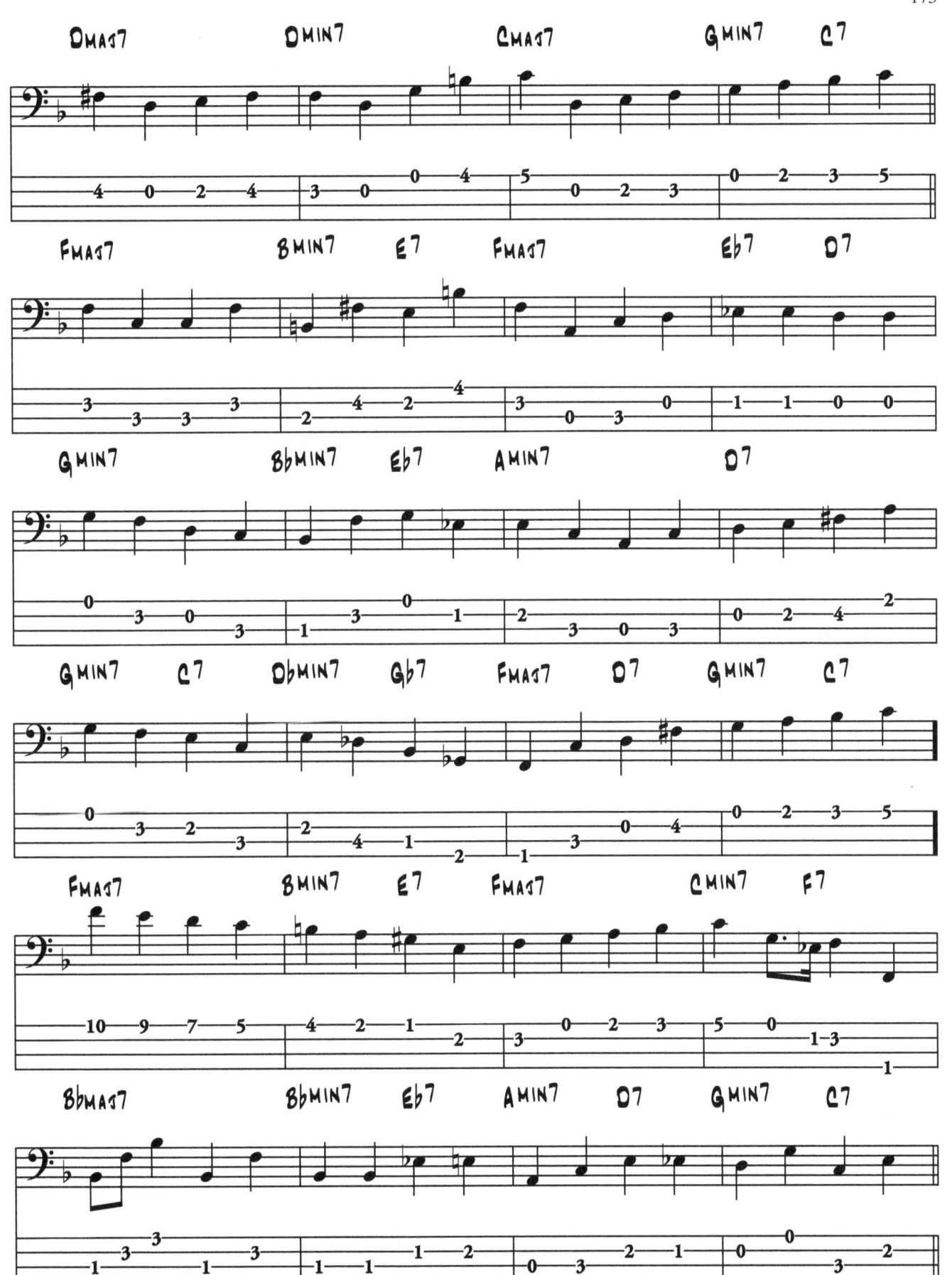

Standard Line Vol.I

Standard Line Vol.I

Standard Line Vol.I

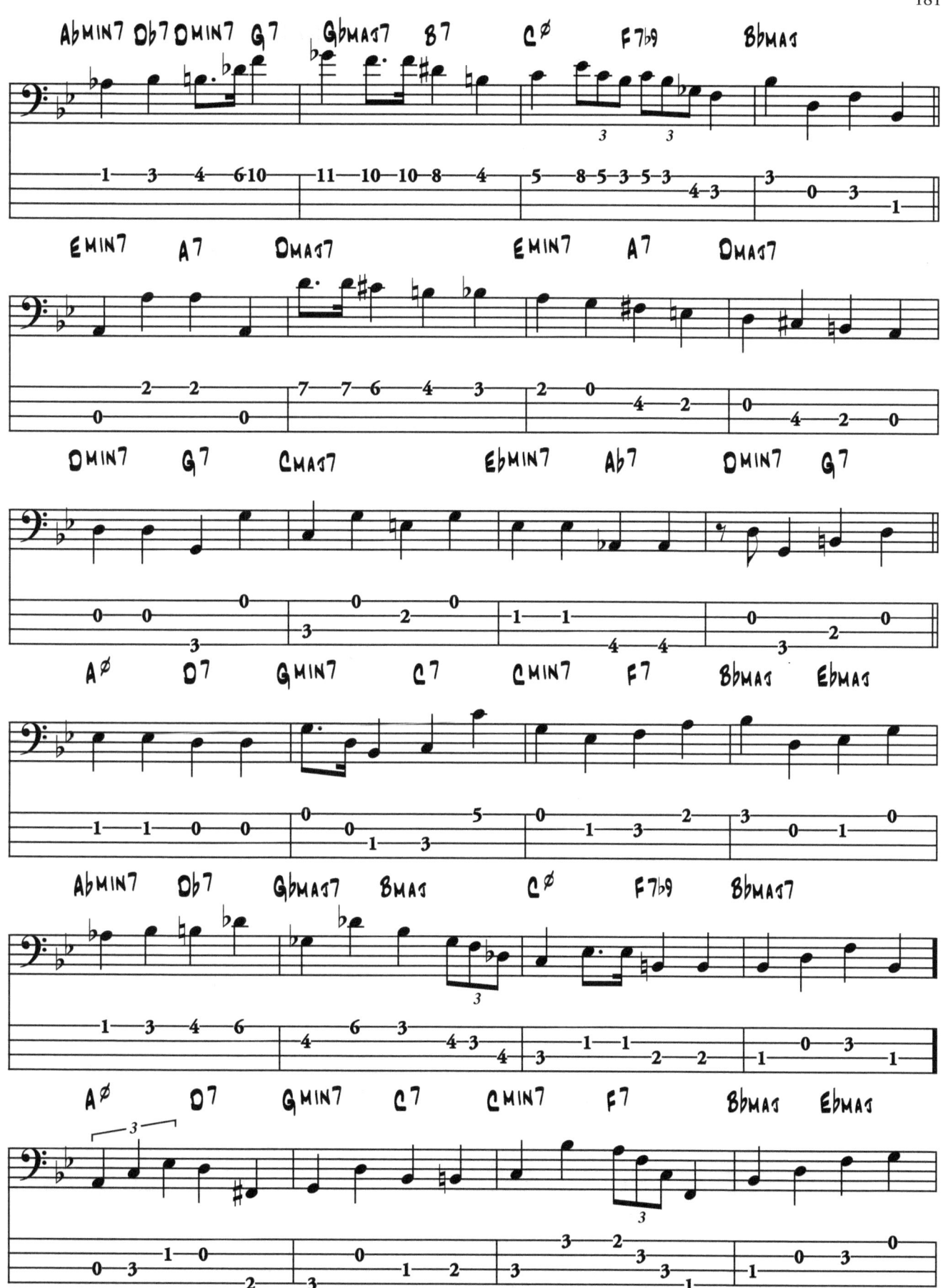

Standard Line Vol.I

Standard Line Vol.I

"THE THIRD" ジャズコード進行 #21

Standard Line Vol.I

©Waterfall Publishing House 2011

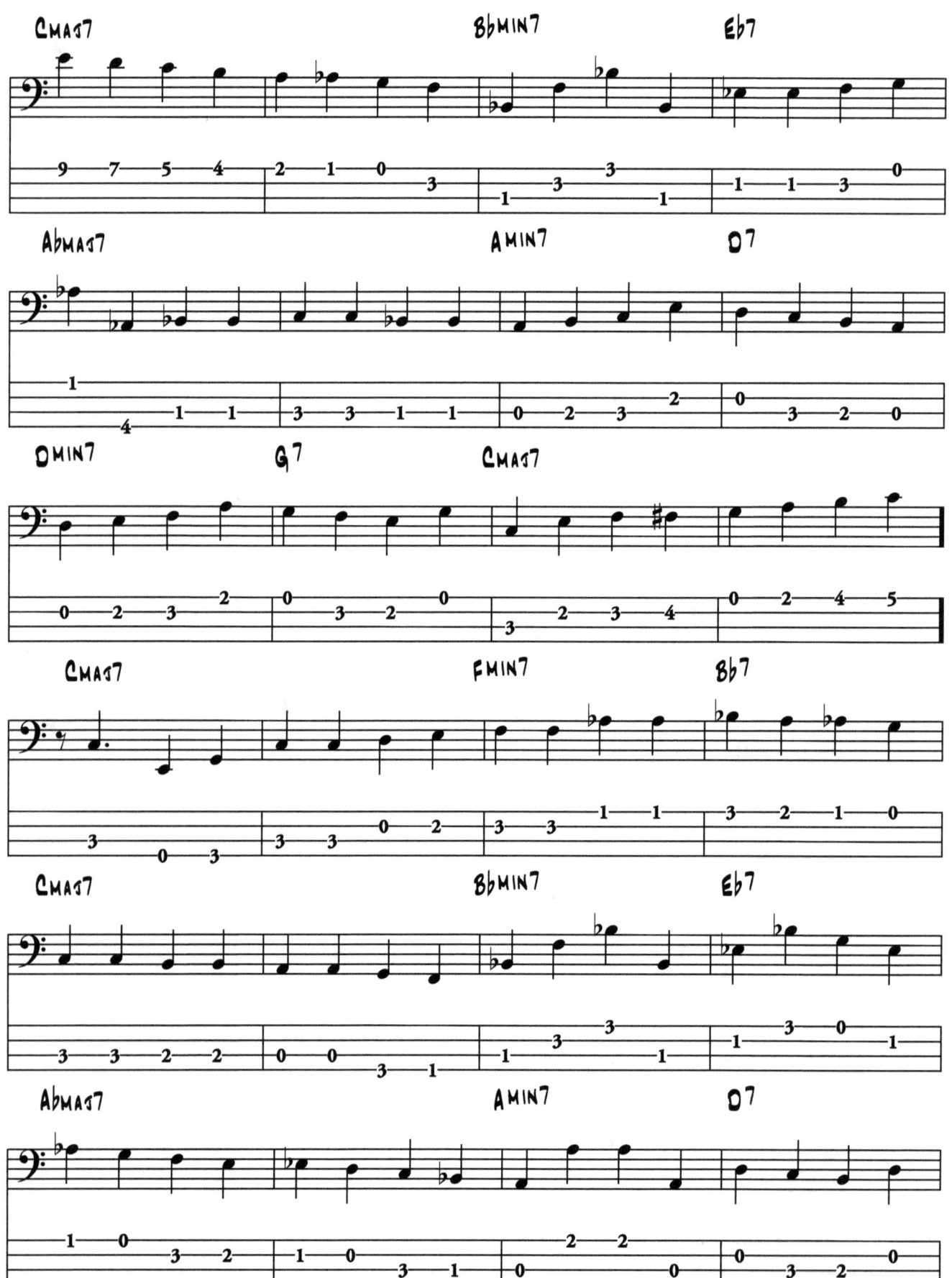

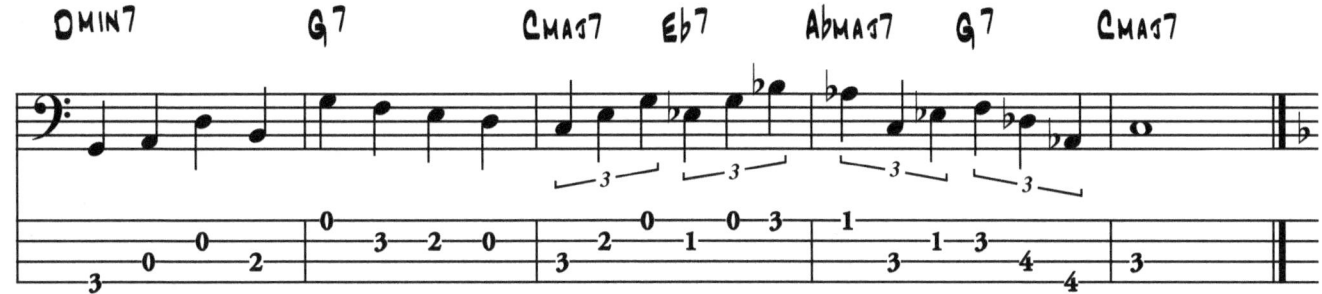

Standard Line Vol.I

Standard Line Vol.I

Standard Line Vol.1

"BRING YOUR STRINGS" ジャズコード進行 #23

©Waterfall Publishing House 2011

Standard Line Vol.I

Standard Line Vol.I

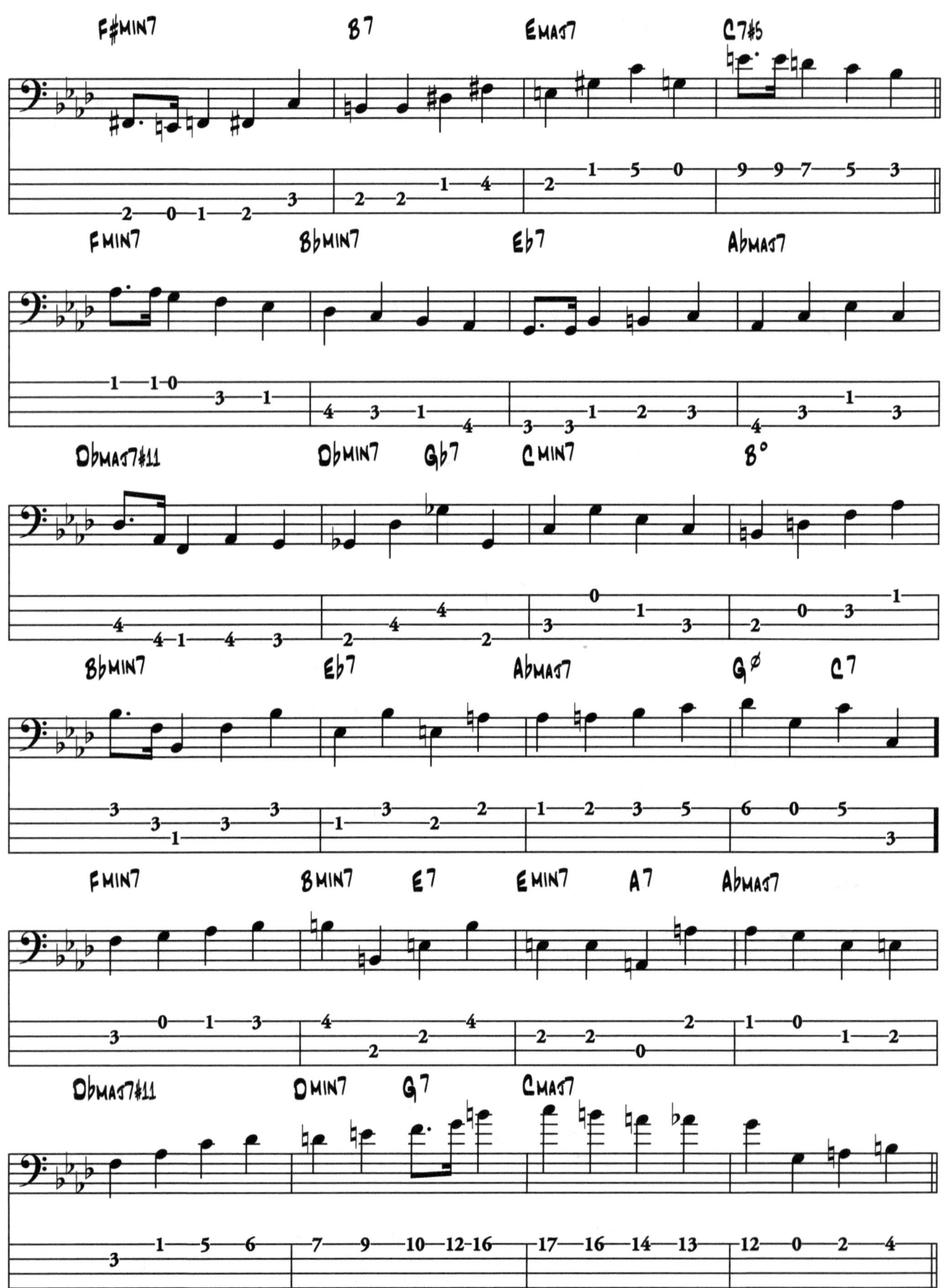

Standard Line Vol.I

©Waterfall Publishing House 2011

"NO ONES HERE" ジャズコード進行 #24

Standard Line Vol.I

Standard Line Vol.I

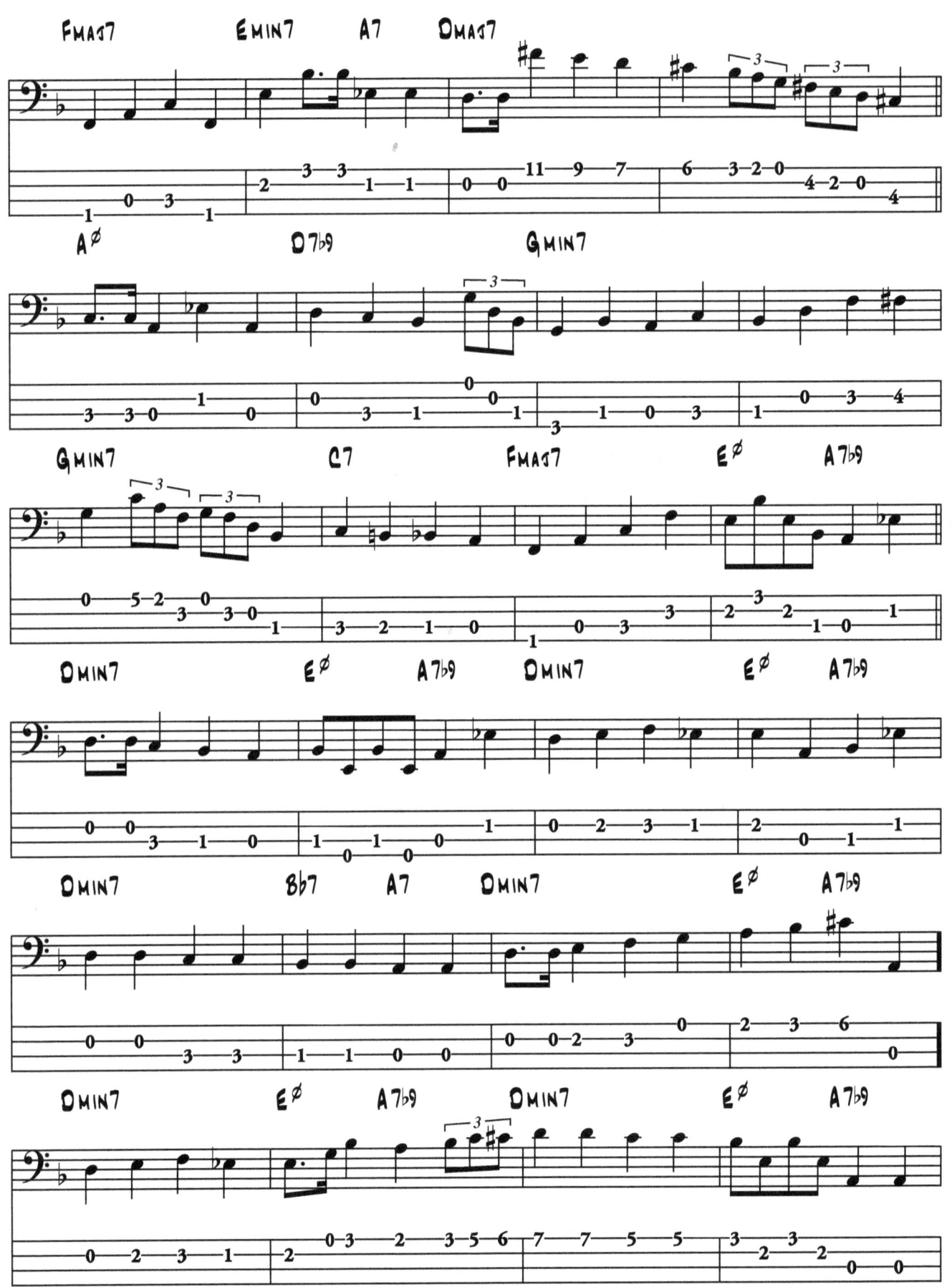

Standard Line Vol.I

Standard Line Vol.I

終わりに臨んで、、、

　これまでに紹介したトピック全ての例を含む、この本の最後のページまで到達するには、多くの量の理解と、集中した練習が必要だったことでしょう。
　この本の目的は、意欲あるベーシストが、どのようにしてメロディーやソロイストをサポートするジャズウォーキングベースラインを作っていくか、ということの理解するために、しっかりとした基礎を養ってもらうことにありました。
　この本のトピックを網羅することで、ベーシストとして、ジャズミュージシャンとして、自己のスタイルを探し始めることができると信じています。
　出来うる限り、多く音楽を聴く時間をもってください。マスターと呼ばれる人たちの演奏を聴きましょう。

備考　　本書では、読者に対して、ジャズにおけるコードシンボルや、読譜に親しんでもらうという観点から、異名同音が使われています。

本書は目的の一つとして、読者が自信を持ってトピック及び演奏例を理解し消化して、次に進めるように、出来る限り分かりやすく書かれています。

本書に関する感想やコメントは、未来の世代のミュージシャンに、質の良い音楽教育素材を提供するという意味からも、私たちにとって大変重要です。

あなたの感想やコメントをconstructwalkingjazzbasslines@gmail.comまでお寄せください。

Standard Line Vol.I

Other books available in this series このシリーズのその他の本

日本語での出版物

コンストラクティング ウォーキング ジャズベースラインズ ブック I
ウォーキング ベースラインズ ブルース in 12 keys

コンストラクティング ウォーキング ジャズベースラインズ ブック II
ウォーキング ベースラインズ リズムチェンジ(循環) in 12 keys

コンストラクティング ウォーキング ジャズベースラインズ ブック III
ウォーキング ベースラインズ スタンダードラインズ

コンストラクティング ウォーキング ジャズベースラインズ ブック IV
(カミングスーン)

ベースタブ譜シリーズ

コンストラクティング ウォーキング ジャズベースラインズ ブック I
ウォーキング ベースラインズ ブルース in 12 keys タブ譜バージョン

コンストラクティング ウォーキング ジャズベースラインズ ブック II
ウォーキング ベースラインズ リズムチェンジ(循環) in 12 keys タブ譜バージョン

コンストラクティング ウォーキング ジャズベースラインズ ブック III
ウォーキング ベースラインズ スタンダードラインズ　タブ譜バージョン

コンストラクティング ウォーキング ジャズベースラインズ ブック IV
タブ譜バージョン　(カミングスーン)

イーブックシリーズ

コンストラクティング ウォーキング ジャズベースラインズ ブック I
ウォーキング ベースラインズ ブルース in 12 keys

コンストラクティング ウォーキング ジャズベースラインズ ブック II
ウォーキング ベースラインズ リズムチェンジ(循環) in 12 keys

コンストラクティング ウォーキング ジャズベースラインズ ブック III
ウォーキング ベースラインズ スタンダードラインズ

コンストラクティング ウォーキング ジャズベースラインズ ブック IV
(カミングスーン)

©Waterfall Publishing House 2011

イーブックシリーズ　続き

ベースタブ譜シリーズ

コンストラクティング ウォーキング ジャズベースラインズ ブック I
ウォーキング ベースラインズ ブルース in 12 keys タブ譜バージョン

コンストラクティング ウォーキング ジャズベースラインズ ブック II
ウォーキング ベースラインズ リズムチェンジ(循環) in 12 keys タブ譜バージョン

コンストラクティング ウォーキング ジャズベースラインズ ブック III
ウォーキング ベースラインズ スタンダードラインズ　タブ譜バージョン

コンストラクティング ウォーキング ジャズベースラインズ ブック IV
タブ譜バージョン　（カミングスーン）

最新のニュース,新刊のお知らせは下記のホームページをご覧下さい。

http://waterfallpublishinghouse.com

http://constructingwalkingjazzbasslines.com

http://basstab.net

　　ウォーターフォールブリッシングハウスはザ ツリー フォー ザ フューチャー オーガニゼーションと提携しています。 (ザ ツリー フォー ザ フューチャー オーガニゼーションのホームページ www.plant-trees.org)。
　　ウォーターフォールパブリッシングハウスは ツリー フォー ザ フューチャー オーガニゼーションのツリー プランティング プログラムを通して コンストラクティング ウォーキング ジャズ ベースライン シリーズの本1冊が 購入される度に世界中に2本の樹を植えています。

©Waterfall Publishing House 2011

©Waterfall Publishing House 2011

www.ingramcontent.com/pod-product-compliance
Lightning Source LLC
Chambersburg PA
CBHW081835170426
43199CB00017B/2738